W9-BTN-075

The **talkSPORT** Book of

World Cup Banter

The **talkSPORT** Book of
World Cup Banter

All the Ammo You'll Need to Settle any Argument

Edited by Bill Borrows

SIMON &
SCHUSTER

London · New York · Sydney · Toronto

A CBS COMPANY

First published in Great Britain
by Simon & Schuster UK Ltd, 2010
A CBS Company

Copyright © 2010 by Bill Borrows

Copyright © 2010 talkSPORT Limited

This book is copyright under the Berne Convention.
No reproduction without permission.
All rights reserved.

The right of Bill Borrows to be identified as the
author of this work has been asserted by him
in accordance with sections 77 and 78 of the
Copyright, Designs and Patents Act, 1988.

1 3 5 7 9 10 8 6 4 2

Simon & Schuster UK Ltd
1st Floor
222 Gray's Inn Road
London
WC1X 8HB

www.simonandschuster.co.uk

Simon & Schuster Australia
Sydney

A CIP catalogue for this book is available
from the British Library.

ISBN: 978-1-84737-878-1

Typeset and designed by
Craig Stevens and Julian Flanders

Printed and bound in Italy by LEGO SpA

Contents

▓ ACKNOWLEDGEMENTS

Wordsmiths and anoraks:
Derek Hammond, Gary Silke and Tom Ellen.

Those without whom:
Jonathan Conway @ Mulcahy Conway Associates, Julian Flanders, Ali Masud and Craig Stevens.

At talkSPORT Towers:
Adam Bullock, Stan Collymore, Moz Dee, Duncan Stafford and Scott Taunton.

Simon & Schuster:
Ian Marshall, Ian Chapman, Jo Edgecombe, Mike Jones and Rory Scarfe.

And thanks to:
all the talkSPORT listeners and readers of talkSPORT magazine who took the time to vote for their Best and Worst England XIs.

All photographs in this book Copyright © Getty Images, except for pages 36, 43, 53, 65, 71, 81, 89, 107, 159 and 176 which were supplied by Derek Hammond and Gary Silke

▦ INTRODUCTION

Welcome to *The talkSPORT Book of World Cup Banter* – the definitive and indispensable guide to the 2010 FIFA World Cup. All World Cup guides say that, of course, but this one is different. This is for real fans: those who can talk about football for hours; those for whom it absolutely matters; those who know how many goals Gary Lineker scored for England – in short, those like the listeners to talkSPORT.

This book has got all the vital information any real football fan needs to get the best out of this year's tournament, such as the low-down on the competing countries and players to watch. But there is so much more. Within the 200 or so pages that follow are amazing stories of great players and games, some of which you will never forget and some you may never have heard about.

There are controversial lists, brilliant pictures and more facts than you can shake a stick at. If you didn't know England won the World Cup in 1966, then this probably isn't the book for you. If you think the 'Cruyff turn' is something to do with motor racing or that the 'Hand of God' was painted by Leonardo – also a talented Brazilian midfielder, of course – then try the cookery section.

When I tell you that the fact that Zaire lined up before their 1974 World Cup games to the strains of 'In the Mood' by Glenn Miller did not make it in to the book, then you can imagine the competition for places. We do, however, reveal why the Americans never really beat us 1-0 in 1950 – still England's biggest 'upset' – and which head of state was fined 400 Euros for celebrating his country's qualification for the 2010 competition.

It's that kind of definitive and indispensable guide to the 2010 FIFA World Cup.

Hope you enjoy it.

Bill Borrows (Editor)

P.S. Oh, and you can follow EVERY game of the 2010 FIFA World Cup live on talkSPORT – with full commentary and expert analysis of all 64 games so you won't miss a single match.

▥ WORLD CUP 2010 VENUES

Green Point Stadium, Cape Town
Gross capacity: 70,000

▪ The exterior of the stadium is covered with 'noise-reducing cladding'. So blow that vuvuzela as loud as you like, because the neighbours can't hear you.

▪ Green Point also boasts a retractable roof, to limit light pollution, which makes it perhaps the most thoughtful football stadium in history.

▪ The late King of Pop, Michael Jackson, performed at the original stadium on the site in October 1997.

▪ The Green Point Common – the site on which the stadium is built – was originally christened 'de Waterplaats' ('The Foreshore') by Dutch settlers in the 18th century, and was regularly used to host sailing regattas.

▪ If this ground were a footballer: Gary Lineker. Considerate, well-behaved, squeaky clean. And, as a result, slightly irritating.

Durban Stadium (aka Moses Mabhida Stadium), Durban
Gross capacity: 70,000

▪ The stadium is named after Moses Mabhida, a politician who was leader of the South African Communist Party from 1978 to 1985.

▪ It boasts a 350m arch stretching up and over the pitch, which reaches its peak 106m above the ground. If you're interested in witnessing the majesty of

The Moses Mabhida Stadium in Durban: the split in the arch takes its design cues from the South African flag.

Durban's panoramic views and shoreline – or you just fancy gobbing on some overpaid sportsmen – you can even take a funicular ride across it.

■ The stadium takes its design cues from the South African flag. Apparently the architects behind the Millennium Stadium had the same idea with the Welsh flag, but had difficulty finding a dragon who'd commit to the project.

■ The layout of the Moses Mabhida Stadium means that Durban is now qualified to host several Olympic disciplines in one venue, which suggests the possibility of a future Olympic or Commonwealth Games bid.

■ If this ground were a footballer: David Beckham. High-flying and useful in a big sporting bid.

Ellis Park Stadium, Johannesburg

Gross capacity: 61,000

■ The ground is named after J.D.Ellis, a Johannesburg city councillor. Coincidentally, he was the very same Johannesburg city councillor who authorised its construction. Wonder how he managed to swing that one?

■ The South African rugby team won the World Cup here in 1995, beating the mighty All Blacks and re-establishing themselves as a force to be reckoned with in the field of oval-shaped ball-tossing.

■ Countries playing at Ellis Park will be pleased to learn that the facilities include 'team whirlpools'. So, by the sounds of it, an early bath might be a bonus.

■ Ellis Park is the home of Premier Soccer League team Orlando Pirates.

■ If this ground were a footballer: Wayne Rooney. Extremely capable but occasionally looks like it might be better suited to rugby.

Soccer City, Johannesburg

Gross capacity: 94,700

■ The design of South Africa's flagship stadium is based on a 'calabash' – a kind of traditional African pot. The stadium's exterior is a huge mosaic of fire and earth, lit up from below by lights, which represent the fire underneath the pot.

■ Soccer City hosted the first mass rally for Nelson Mandela, following his release from Robben Island in 1990.

■ South Africa won the African Cup of Nations here in 1996, beating Tunisia 2-0 in the final.

■ The ground is currently the largest stadium construction site in the world and employs 3,000 staff.

■ If this ground were a footballer: Kaká. Breathtaking, glamorous, one of the greatest in the world. The only drawback is the ridiculous name.

Free State Stadium, Mangaung, Bloemfontein

Gross capacity: 48,000

■ The stadium is home to Premier Soccer League side Bloemfontein Celtic, who were named after the Scottish side in 1984 and also share their green/white colours. Siwelele – the Celtic fans – are widely known as the most passionate in the country.

■ Free State hosted the hugely entertaining 2009 Confederations Cup semi-final, in which USA dumped European champions Spain out of the competition in style with a dramatic 2-0 victory.

■ The city is renowned for its abundance of colourful roses, and in Dutch 'Bloemfontein' means 'fountain of flowers'. In Sesotho, however, the city is known as Mangaung, which translates as 'place of cheetahs'. So, don't get too comfortable.

■ New Zealand gave poor old Japan something of a mauling here in the 1995 Rugby World Cup, defeating them 145-17.

■ If this ground were a footballer: Henrik Larsson. Stylish, exciting, beloved by Celtic supporters.

Nelson Mandela Bay Stadium, Nelson Mandela Bay, Port Elizabeth

Gross capacity: 48,000

■ The stadium is nicknamed 'The Sunflower' due to the rows of huge white 'petals' that make up its roof.

■ One of the first major test events at the Nelson Mandela Bay Stadium was the infamous Soweto derby between Orlando Pirates and Kaizer Chiefs – a clash which regularly attracts capacity crowds.

■ In November 2009, the stadium hosted the Miss World Sports event of the Miss World 2009 pageant.

The staff at the Nelson Mandela Bay Stadium cut costs by employing ants to take their publicity photos.

■ Nelson Mandela Bay, Port Elizabeth, is known in South Africa as 'The Friendly City'. If you happen to be mugged there, feel free to remind your assailant of this fact.

■ If this ground were a footballer: Cristiano Ronaldo. Has managed to attract scores of beautiful women, despite overtly feminine appearance.

Mbombela Stadium, Nelspruit

Gross capacity: 46,000

■ The Mbombela Stadium is situated near several game parks, including the Kruger National Park and the Jane Goodall Chimpanzee Eden. The roof supports at the Mbombela Stadium all resemble giraffes in honour of this fact.

■ Most of South Africa's avocados and citrus fruits are grown in the areas surrounding this stadium.

■ 'Mbombela' is a siSwati word (siSwati being one of the 11 official South African languages) meaning 'many people together in a small space'.

■ Construction of the Mbombela was marred by violent protests by local people angry at the failure to replace the two schools which were demolished to make way for the stadium.

■ If this ground were a footballer: Joey Barton. Continues to function in football, despite major protests.

Peter Mokaba Stadium, Polokwane

Gross capacity: 46,000

■ The Peter Mokaba Stadium replaces another Peter Mokaba Stadium situated on the same spot, after plans to upgrade the old one were abandoned in favour of a complete rebuild.

■ Ivory Coast's Didier Drogba made his international debut against South Africa in 2002 at the old Peter Mokaba Stadium, in an African Cup of Nations qualifying match. The home side ended up winning 2-1. Didier, we presume, ended up writhing about on the floor, holding his ankle.

■ Peter Mokaba himself was a Polokwane-born member of South African Parliament, who was active in opposing the apartheid government throughout the 1980s.

■ The stadium's design is based on the Baobab – an iconic African tree. If you fancy seeing one of these huge specimens in the flesh [shouldn't that be 'bark'? – Ed], why not pop down to The Big Baobab Pub near the ground – a fully licensed bar situated inside the hollow 155ft circumference of a Baobab trunk.

■ If this ground were a footballer: Peter Crouch. Both called Peter, both designed to resemble trees.

Royal Bafokeng Stadium, Rustenburg

Gross capacity: 42,000

■ The Royal Bafokeng Stadium is named after the Bafokeng people, who live in the surrounding area. Rustenburg is home to the two largest platinum mines in the world and, in 1999, the Bafokeng won a legal battle that entitled them to 20 percent of the platinum mined on their land.

■ Despite the fact that Rustenburg does not have its own team, many Premier Soccer League games are still played at the stadium.

■ Luxury casino resort Sun City is located on the outskirts of Rustenburg. The resort's golf course famously boasts a hole with a water feature containing 38 real crocodiles. Worrying for caddies; amusing for everyone else.

■ South Africa's famous 21-20 defeat of the All Blacks took place here in September 2006.

■ If this ground were a footballer: Craig Bellamy. Faced legal action in the past and authorities are concerned that its proximity to golf clubs may distract from its huge footballing talent.

Bellamy without club. Which is odd, because he has had almost 276,429 of them.

Loftus Versfeld Stadium, Tshwane, Pretoria

Gross capacity: 50,000

■ The stadium takes its name from Robert Owen Loftus Versfeld, the founder of organised sports in Pretoria.

■ South Africa's first-ever victory over a European footballing side took place here, when they beat Sweden 1-0 back in 1999.

■ Worried about having a good time in Pretoria? Well, stop worrying! The city is home to the Post Office Museum; a museum dedicated – as you may have guessed – to the history and development of the South African postal services. Exhibits include telephones, telegraphs and even stamps. Yes, even stamps. Why even bother going to the game?

■ The site has been used for major sporting events since 1903. The first concrete stadium on the site held just 2,000 spectators.

■ If this ground were a footballer: Ryan Giggs. Still going strong, despite being over a hundred years old.

★ ★ ★

▦ TALKING A GOOD GAME

Scotland's Denis Law makes alternative arrangements to avoid watching England's World Cup final, in *The King* (2003)

So there we were on the golf course, and I was trying to concentrate on my game knowing that some of my mates were playing the biggest game of their lives. Again my mate gave me a thrashing, I lost my £25 bet, and as we rounded the corner from the last, heading towards the clubhouse, all the members were standing outside holding up four fingers for the four goals with one hand, and a pint in the other.

▦ FALSE START
MAKING THE WORLD CUP

1904 ▪ Seven national representatives meet in Paris to form FIFA, and come up with the brainwave of staging a world football tournament separate from the Olympics.

1906 ▪ An attempt is made by FIFA to stage an international tournament in Switzerland. Matches are actually played, but the event is a shambles.

1908 ▪ Hold on, this is easy! FIFA manages to arrange a football tournament at the 1908 London Olympics. England win!

1909 ▪ The Sir Thomas Lipton Trophy is arranged in Italy by – yes, you know who – involving club teams from Italy, Germany and Switzerland. But the FA doesn't want English clubs to take part. West Auckland, an amateur side from County Durham, travel in place of the big boys... and win!

1911 ▪ West Auckland win the Sir Thomas Lipton Trophy again! And yes, that is Lipton as in Lipton's Tea.

1920 ▪ At FIFA's Antwerp Congress, president Jules Rimet and secretary Henri Delaunay remember the decent idea

Quite what Fatty Arbuckle* was doing receiving a trophy from Jules Rimet, a man with his name 'quite literally' on the cup, was always a mystery.
* It is not Arbuckle, Fatty but Dr Jude, Rotund of the Uruguayan FA.

they had 16 years ago. So, let's stage an inter-continental cup competition, eh? Like we just did for the very first time at the 1920 Olympics (which, not coincidentally, were held in Antwerp!).

1924

■ FIFA is encouraged by the success of the football competition at the 1924 Paris Olympics, which proves once again that its big idea is do-able.

1928

■ Right then. Hungary as host country, agreed? It'll be the first ever FIFA World Cup. But unforeseen complications lie in wait. Only four countries end up making the trip, and the tournament ends in utter failure. Maybe it wasn't such a great idea to try to stage the tournament in Olympic year, eh?

1930

■ The inaugural FIFA World Cup finally takes place in Uruguay, the country that won the Olympic title in 1924 and 1928. However, only two of the founder members – France and Belgium – can be bothered to make the trip. Netherlands, Italy, Sweden and Spain have got the arse because their bids failed. And, by this time, all four home countries have withdrawn from FIFA over a squabble about amateurism. Roll on 1950...

Uruguay win the first ever World Cup, Montevideo 1930.

▦ WHAT THE PAPERS SAY
1930 WORLD CUP

Given the glut of media coverage for the World Cup nowadays, one could be forgiven for thinking it was ever thus. In fact, it used to be very different. The first World Cup tournament was almost completely ignored by the British press. None of the home nations was a member of FIFA and they looked down their noses at the first faltering attempt to organise a global tournament. The national newspapers didn't even comment on the final, with the exception of two column inches in the *Manchester Guardian* on 31 July 1930:

'Scenes exceeding in enthusiasm even those of an English Cup final were witnessed here today, when 100,000 people assembled to watch Uruguay and the Argentine meet in the final of the so-called world's Association football championship. Twenty special trains unloaded thousands of people from up country, and fleets of aeroplanes brought spectators from remote towns. All the shops and offices in the city were closed, and business was at a standstill. Among the early arrivals were 50 members of parliament. It will be recalled that Uruguay and Argentine fought out the Olympic final at Amsterdam in 1928, when, after a draw, Uruguay won by two to one. Uruguay won to-day by four goals to three.'

Just 115 words – and they got the score wrong.

★ ★ ★

▦ STAN COLLYMORE'S ULTIMATE AND IMPOSSIBLE WORLD CUP PUB QUIZ

1 When did England play their first-ever World Cup match? Who was it against? And where?

2 How did Scotland fare in their first World Cup game? Clue: it was a ten-goal thriller.

3 How many times has the reigning FIFA Player of the Year been in the World Cup-winning team?

4 Why could France's manager from the 1938 finals said to have been 'dancing with the captain'?

5 How many Uruguayans died as a result of their team's 1930 World Cup win – and how did they perish?

6 He was stripped and ready to go with minutes remaining to kick-off. So why did Rajko Metic fail to make the team versus Brazil in 1950, forcing the Yugoslavians to play with ten men before a Maracana crowd of 142,409?

7 Which England player sparked controversy by appearing to be the worse for wear on disembarkation from the team plane at Mexico 1970?

Bobby: 'I'm telling you Jack, this is the future.' Jack: 'Just shave it off. You look like a right twat.'

8 Which team attempted to steal the courtesy luxury coach provided by a German company for the 1974 finals?

9 What happened when the Dutch referee blew the whistle for the re-start after half time of Morocco-West Germany, at Mexico 1970?

10 What was the reffing controversy that made a mockery of the Argentina-France group game at the 1930 World Cup?

11 How many electricity plants were wrecked by Bangladeshi football fans after a power cut interrupted live TV coverage of the USA-Switzerland opener at USA 1994?

Sub Belgian ref John Langenus insisted on the crowd being searched on entry to the 1930 World Cup final between Uruguay and Argentina. What did the search turn up?

Answers on page 204

⠿ VITAL PUB INFO
TO FOSTER FRIENDLY RELATIONS WITH FANS OF

SOUTH AFRICA

Fanspotter's guide

They sound a lot like Aussies, with accents best imitated by wearing hundreds of elastic bands around the lower face and jaw. A yellow shirt will help, too. And that's 'Bafana bafana' they're shouting, by the way, not 'Banana Banana'.

Conversation starter

Fancy some *skop*? [A popular dish made from the head of a cow, sheep or goat. Once scrubbed to remove the skin, ears and nose, it's then boiled and simmered. And then eaten. And then, presumably, thrown up again several minutes later.]

Accentuate the positive

They've got home advantage.

Skirt expertly around the negative

Look at what Japan and Korea achieved back in 2002.

Form guide

Came fourth in the 2009 Confederations Cup, but the biggest scalp they claimed was that of New Zealand. Did not qualify for the 2010 African Cup of Nations.

One to watch

Ex-Ajax *wunderkind* Benni McCarthy plays for West Ham United, but he's now 32, and enjoyed his best years at Celta Vigo and Porto. Captain Aaron Mokoena is one of several middling European-based pros in the team, but there doesn't look much class among the players from the domestic Premier Soccer League.

Simply the best... ever

Lucas Radebe, popular Leeds United stopper who moved for £250,000 from the Kaizer Chiefs. Made 70 utterly solid international appearances up to 2003, scoring two goals.

Useful Afrikaans phrases

Is jy n' bewonderaar Van die Kaizer Chiefs? – Are you a fan of the Kaizer Chiefs? *Het jy vind dit vreemd dat Steven Pienaar 'n geskeer haar lyn in die voorkant van sy cornrows het? Hoekom hou hy nie maak sy gedagtes aan? Óf skeer jou kop het of cornrows. Moenie sit op die heining nie* – Do you find it strange that Steven Pienaar has a shaved hairline before his cornrows start? Why doesn't he make his mind up? Either shave your head, or have cornrows. Don't sit on the fence.

Chat-up line
I'd be happy to achieve even 50 percent of the greatness of a figure such as your Mandela. I certainly wouldn't mind getting you in a half-nelson.

This one's on me
Pinotage/Hanepoort – wines made from specially cultivated grape from the Cape area. Or Rooibos tea.

Inside line on South African culture
Sangomas [a type of shaman] are very common in South Africa. In many towns, they will even distribute pamphlets advertising their services, which promise everything from more impressive sexual performance to the winning lottery numbers. Many football teams also have their own resident witch doctor. Their duties include sprinkling urine over the goalposts before kick-off and burying bundles of herbs underneath the pitch. So, similar to those of a fourth official, then.

Common ground
Four of the five fastest creatures in the world live in South Africa: the cheetah (70mph), wildebeest, lion and Thomson's gazelle. The fifth – Gabby Agbonlahor – lives in Solihull.

★ ★ ★

▦ TALKING A GOOD GAME

Brazil's Ronaldo,
after the quarter-final
against England, 2002

> Normally when you swap shirts they are soaked in sweat, but Beckham's smelt of perfume. Either he protects himself against BO or he sweats cologne.

▦ WORLD CUP SONGS
ENGLAND 1966

Lonnie Donegan – 'World Cup Willie'
(Failed to chart)
John Peel always rated groundbreaking rocker Lonnie Donegan as England's own Elvis, but just like The King he was some way off the pace by the Swinging mid-60s. The first song ever to get FIFA's official World Cup stamp was a scuffling trad-jazz workout with music-hall lyrics – 'We're all football crazy / And it's plain to see / That we're all so happy / Like one big familee' – devoted to the tournament's personality-free lion mascot.

MEXICO 1970

England World Cup Squad – 'Back Home'
(Number 1)
Right from the big cha-cha cha-cha-cha intro (borrowed, incidentally, from 'You'll Never Walk Alone', the synth-crazed flipside of Cliff Portwood's 'Up There England'), this horn-driven romp epitomises everything a World Cup song should be. Jeff Astle's finest moment leading

Check out the soundman just in front of Gordon Banks. He seems to think the song is going to be a winner. That or Nobby Stiles' mic is not plugged in.

the line for England stirs and bonds: while we're watching them on the box, they're thinking about us, the folks back home. Forget your arsey postmodern irony: jut your chin and fight back the tears.

★ ★ ★

▦ WHAT THE PAPERS SAY
1962 WORLD CUP

The build-up to Chile was covered in detail by *Charles Buchan's Football Monthly* (price 1/6). The magazine celebrated England's qualification for the tournament with this report of the match against Portugal:

THROUGH TO THE FINALS

Oct. 25 1961 · World Cup Qualifying Round, Second Leg (Wembley)
England booked her passage to Chile and the World Cup finals next June in the first ten minutes of this game. But a 100,000 crowd which returned an English record for receipts – £52,500 – had little to cheer for the rest of the afternoon.

Three times the Portuguese forwards rattled the English woodwork. Twice an unusually nervy Springett had to dive again to complete his save at the second attempt. And even Haynes found few loopholes in a well-ordered defence. The lanky, 19-year-old Eusebio, at inside-right for Portugal, was the game's star attacker, being way above anybody in the disappointing England forward line.

Last season's fluency of movement has still to be recaptured by the English team. The defence has been strengthened by the inclusion of Wilson, but the attack presents problems. On this form there is some way to go before home followers can get excited about England's chances in Chile.

England: Springett (Sheff Wed); Armfield (Blackpool); Wilson (Huddersfield); Robson (West Brom); Swan (Sheff Wed); Flowers (Wolves); Connelly (Burnley); Douglas (Blackburn); Pointer (Burnley); Haynes (Fulham); Charlton (Man U).

ENGLAND 2 (Connelly, Pointer), **PORTUGAL 0**

★ ★ ★

▦ PROLIFERATION OF SLIGHTLY CRAP AWARDS

1970

■ FIFA Fair Play Trophy For the team with the best record of fair play, which in its inaugural year went to Peru. A belated 'fair played, amigos' to the boys in the over-the-shoulder stripes.

1982

■ Golden Boot For the top goalscorer. Was applied retrospectively to all tournaments from 1930.

■ Golden Ball For the 'outstanding player' at each finals. A shortlist is drawn up by the FIFA technical committee, and the winner is voted for by representatives of the media. This was also applied retrospectively to all tournaments from 1930.

1990

■ All-Star Team Commercially sponsored Best XI of the tournament.

1994

■ Silver Shoe and Bronze Shoe Like the Golden Boot, introduced so the not-so-high goalscorers wouldn't feel left out on the metallic slipper front.

■ The Yashin Award For the best goalkeeper. It was named after Russia's all-time best Number 1, Lev.

■ The Most Entertaining Team Chosen by public poll, now takes place on FIFAworldcup.com. Let's all vote for New Zealand!

2006

■ The Best Young Player Award According to those busybodies at the FIFA Technical Study Group.

★ ★ ★

VITAL PUB INFO
TO FOSTER FRIENDLY RELATIONS WITH FANS OF

MEXICO

Fanspotter's guide

Green shirt, beeg hat. If you happen to be in an elevated position in the pub, your new Mexican friends will look a bit like fried eggs. And may well be riding a bike.

Conversation starter

Le ganamos a usted mucho 8-0 en 1961. Simplemente decir, eso es todo – We beat you lot 8-0 back in 1961. Just saying, that's all.

Accentuate the positive

Not a lot of people know that Sven-Göran Eriksson coached Mexico during the early qualification rounds. A man with a quality CV in World Cup coaching.

Skirt expertly around the negative

It was only once he'd been sacked and replaced by Javier Aguirre that the Mexicans kicked on by taking 16 points from seven games and ensured qualification, as usual, alongside the US.

Form guide

Coming together nicely – including a recent run of 12 unbeaten – and must stand a chance in a group with a weak seed (namely hosts South Africa) alongside France and Uruguay.

One to watch

Midfield general and regular goalscorer Cuauhtémoc Blanco may be 36, but having been coaxed out of international retirement by coach Aguirre, he was inspirational in the qualifiers.

Simply the best… ever

Hugo Sanchez – three World Cups (1978, 86, 94), 12 seasons in the Spanish Primera División, five Pichichis (top goalscorer trophy), four of them consecutively (1985-88 inclusive).

Useful Spanish phrases

¿Por qué el gusano en el tequila? Usted no me ven pegar una tijereta en mi Foster's – Why the worm in the tequila? You don't see me sticking an earwig in my Foster's.

¿Cuál es la diferencia oficial entre un burrito y una enchilada? – What is the official difference between a burrito and an enchilada?

Chat-up line

Let's make like it's 3 February. [Carnaval, a five-day celebration of the libido, is held on this date before the Catholic Lent.]

This one's on me

Tequila. Worm optional.

Inside line on Mexican culture

In Mexico, 1 November is The Day of the Dead, a festival dedicated to the remembrance of friends and family members who have passed away. The marches and parades are a fearsome spectacle – thousands of crazed revellers, decked out in black capes and skull masks.

Common ground

Mexico introduced the world to chocolate, corn and chillies. According to its cultural advisors, the country's next major goal is to introduce the world to something that doesn't begin with the letter C.

★ ★ ★

▦ RIGHT NAME, WRONG COUNTRY

- Italia (Brazil, 1930)
- Luigi Allemandi (Italy, 1934)
- Alfonso Portugal (Mexico, 1958)
- Americo (Portugal, 1966)
- Germano (Portugal, 1966)
- Rinus Israel (Netherlands, 1974)
- Joe Jordan (Scotland, 1974)
- Guy Francois (Haiti, 1974)
- Bob Mali (Jamaica, 1978)
- Alan Brazil (Scotland, 1982)
- Miguel Espana (Mexico, 1986)
- Carlos Germano (Brazil, 1998)
- German Villa (Mexico, 1998)
- Matt Holland (Republic of Ireland, 2002)
- Jason Scotland (Trinidad & Tobago, 2006)

And there goes the Big Man. Alan Brazil in his pomp. Hang on a minute, where has he gone? Alan? Alan?

WHATEVER HAPPENED TO THE HEROES?

Marcel Desailly • France 1998, 2002

Late in 2009, the 1998 World Cup and Euro 2000 winner hit the headlines for his work in Ghana, where he now provides a home and an education for children detached from their families. In Ghana, meanwhile, it made just as big a splash when Desailly twice turned down the chance to manage the Black Stars at the 2010 World Cup. In his club career, he won the Champions League with Olympique Marseille and Milan before moving to Chelsea for £4.6 million in 1998, and kept up the good work for six years. He won 116 caps for France and is now a UNICEF ambassador and popular pundit. Top man!

Lucien Laurent • France 1930

An amateur playing for the semi-pro outfit Cercle Athlétique de Paris, Laurent only picked up expenses for his trip to Uruguay for the first World Cup finals. Only 1,000 fans turned up for the inaugural match against the hosts, still providing a far greater fanfare than Laurent received in France. 'I remember when I got home, there was just a tiny mention in one of the papers. Football was only in its infancy.' And yet the car factory worker and future bar owner had made history by volleying home the first ever World Cup goal – 'nothing special', in his own words. He was crocked in the second game against Argentina, and had to wait 68 years for his next big moment – wowing the world's assembled media with his memories as the only surviving member of the 1930 side – and watching France beat Brazil 3-0 in the 1998 final.

Felipe Ramos Rizo • Referee, Mexico 2002

He was the ref who harshly sent off Ronaldinho for a mistimed tackle on Danny Mills in the England-Brazil quarter-final of 2002. He could have been English football's all-time hero, had Brazil's ten men not somehow upped a gear and cruised to victory.

Having reffed his first match in 1983, aged 20, the Mexican was nearing the end of a long career when he gained notice as one of the pickiest officials at Japan/South Korea 2002, flashing eleven yellow and three red cards in three matches. On the FIFA list from 1997 until retirement in 2003, he earlier sparked controversy in the 2000 Olympic final, dismissing two Spanish players. Now a Mexican TV pundit, Felipe runs his own eponymous referees' association and academy, with his website ramosrizo.com.mx clocking up more than five million hits.

⠿ TEENAGE KICKS XI

1 Lee Chan-Myung, 19 • North Korea Teenage goalkeepers are extremely rare, but this one managed to keep a clean sheet for North Korea against Italy in 1966.

2 Giuseppe Bergomi, 18 • Italy The only player to make the youngest and oldest XI, Bergomi was just 18 when he helped Italy to the title in Spain in 1982.

3 Manuel Rosos, 18 • Mexico Defender who became the youngest-ever World Cup scorer when he converted a penalty for Mexico against Argentina in 1930.

4 Edu, 16 • Brazil The midfielder was just 16 years old when selected for the squad travelling to England in 1966, but he did not make a World Cup appearance until 1970.

5 Elías Figueroa, 19 • Chile Played in all three of Chile's games in 1966 and went on to captain his country.

6 Norman Whiteside, 17 – Northern Ireland Manchester United's starlet took Pelé's record away, becoming the youngest player ever to appear in a World Cup finals. He was just 17 years and 41 days when he lined up for Northern Ireland against Yugoslavia in their Group 5 game in 1982. He played in all five of Northern Ireland's games, including the shock 1-0 win over hosts Spain.

7 Theo Walcott, 17 • England Walcott was Sven-Göran Eriksson's surprise inclusion in the England squad that travelled to Germany in 2006, but didn't get a game.

8 Martin Hoffmann, 19 • East Germany The striker played in six games in the 1974 tournament, scoring once.

9 Michael Owen, 18 • England Owen was just 18 years old when he scored his wonder goal against Argentina in the second round.

10 Pelé, 17 • Brazil Became the (then) youngest-ever player in a World Cup tournament in 1958, and then the youngest-ever scorer when he netted for Brazil against Wales during the same tournament.

11 Lionel Messi, 18 • Argentina The Barça star scored the last goal in the 6–0 victory over Serbia and was the youngest scorer in the 2006 tournament.

Friends were concerned that Lionel was taking his *West Ham Anthems* CD too literally.

▦ VITAL PUB INFO
TO FOSTER FRIENDLY RELATIONS WITH FANS OF

URUGUAY

Fanspotter's guide

There are only four million Uruguayans, and it seems every one of them has got a silky light blue shirt. The four stars on the team badge represent World Cup victories in 1930 and 1950, and two early Olympic wins.

Conversation starter

Uruguay and England are the only countries with 100 percent records in World Cup final matches.

Accentuate the positive

Uruguay were the winners of a record 18 international tournaments in the 20th century.

Skirt expertly around the negative

This is the 21st century.

Form guide

Came fifth in South American qualifying, and were forced to the wire in a play-off against CONCACAF's Costa Rica. They won 1-0 away and held on for a 1-1 draw at home in a buttock-clenching thriller!

Three to watch

There are few more competitive, combative defenders in world football than Fenerbahçe's Diego Lugano; another high-impact Uruguayan playing in Europe is free-scoring Ajax winger Luis Suarez. Best keep an eye on Diego Forlan, too, because surely the 2005 and 2009 European Golden Shoe winner can't be as bad as we remember.

Simply the best… ever

Enzo Francescoli is Zinédine Zidane's all-time idol: he even named his son after him. 'El Principe' ('The Prince'), a superb slick string-puller, played 72 times for Uruguay between 1982 and 1997, turning out at club level for Argentina's River Plate, Olympique Marseille (the Zizou link), Cagliari and Torino.

Useful Spanish phrases

Si alguna vez volar sobre los Andes, asegúrese de que no terminan recibiendo comida por el equipo uruguayo de rugby – If you ever fly over the Andes, make sure you don't end up getting eaten by the Uruguayan rugby team.

¡Viva Peñarol/Nacional! Yo se burlan de los torpes, los pasos de tango femenino de la Nacional/Peñarol infieles! – Up the City/United! I sneer at the clumsy, girlish tango steps of the United/City infidels!

Chat-up line

I've seen *The Full Monty* on video, but now I'm far more interested in seeing The Full Montevideo...

This one's on me

Yerba maté is a kind of holly – a pick-me-up that Uruguayans drink like tea, through a metal straw from a hollow gourd.

Inside line on Uruguayan culture

One third of people smoke in Uruguay, but not the country's socialist President, Tabaré Vázquez. Clearly ahead of the game on several counts, he's a doctor specialising in cancer treatment.

Common ground

Montevideo giants Club Atlético Peñarol were founded as Central Uruguay Railway Cricket Club by British railway workers.

★ ★ ★

▦ IT'S ALL GONE OFF
(PART ONE) THE MATCHES

With so much at stake, the World Cup has had some fiery encounters. The following are our favourite five:

The Battle of Berne, 1954

When the quarter-final matched Hungary and Brazil, the two greatest sides in the competition, a fine exhibition of football was anticipated. What unfolded was a hugely violent match that ended in an ugly brawl. Hungary went 2-0 up early on, then Brazil pulled a goal back from a penalty. Towards the end of the first half, the game began to deteriorate into a series of niggling and increasingly more dangerous fouls. In the second half, Hungary made it 3-1, then Brazil pulled a goal back. Amid the tension, Brazil's Nilton Santos fouled József Bozsik and the pair exchanged several punches, before referee Arthur Ellis (later of *It's a Knockout* fame) sent them both off.

Djalma Santos then pursued Zoltán Czibor around the field before the Hungarians made it 4-2. A third player was then dismissed, Humberto Tozzi of Brazil, for kicking Gyula Lóránt. They were just warming up, however. As the players left the field, Pinheiro was hit on the head by a bottle, suffering a bad cut. Some eyewitness accounts claim that it was Ferenc Puskas (who hadn't played in the game) who did this, while others thought it was a spectator. The incensed Brazilians went to their dressing room, got tooled-up with bottles, and then launched an invasion of the Hungarian dressing room which ended in a vicious fight which left one Hungarian unconscious, and the coach badly cut.

The Battle of Santiago, 1962

Chile and Italy met in the Estadio Nacional, Santiago, on 2 June, in a Group 2 game, with the Chilean nation outraged by some unsavoury comments about their capital by a pair of Italian journalists. It didn't take long for the powder keg to go up. In the fifth minute, Italy's Giorgio Ferrini fouled Honorino Landa, and was kicked in retaliation as he lay on the floor. He booted another Chilean in the knee, causing him to collapse on the floor. While English referee Ken Aston was trying to contain this incident, another Italian jabbed an opponent hard in the eye. He went down too. Moments later, as play resumed, Ferrini volleyed another passing Chilean and was sent off. He refused to leave until a dozen policemen came on the field and ushered him off.

In a later incident by the corner flag, Italian Mario David had two hacks at Leonel Sanchez before the Chilean knocked him spark out with a textbook left hook. Sanchez wasn't dismissed for this, but David exacted his own retribution soon after, leaping six feet in the air to kick Sanchez in the back of his head. David was sent off, but it hardly seemed punishment enough.

Some football broke out for a while late on, with Chile taking a 2-0 lead against nine men, but the game ended with several running battles going on. At one point Aston was floored trying to break up a fight, and Sanchez recovered sufficiently to break Humberto Maschio's nose with another smart left. The police had to intervene three more times before Aston blew the final whistle. He started to walk towards the tunnel and then had to come running back to break up a 15-man brawl. Things were different in the good old days...

When Frankie Met Rudi, 1990

Twenty-one minutes into a second-round game between the Netherlands and West Germany in Milan, Frank Rijkaard was booked for a foul on Rudi Voeller. The Dutch defender didn't take this at all well and spat into the German striker's curly mullet as he jogged past him. A row ensued in which Rijkaard gave the international signal for 'You're all yap'. The ref then booked Voeller, who turned round and showed him the glistening evidence. When the free-kick was eventually delivered into the box, Voeller jumped in on goalkeeper Hans van Breukelen, who reacted angrily. Luckily Rijkaard was on hand to help up Voeller – by his ear. As Rijkaard, van Breukelen and Voeller shouted at each other from point-blank range, Juergen Klinsmann came in to break it up but knocked over his team-mate. The ref had had enough by now and showed both Rijkaard and Voeller the red card. Rijkaard then spat in Voeller's hair again as he ran past him towards the tunnel. The Germans had the last laugh, winning 2-1 and dumping the Dutch out of the tournament.

Argie Bargy, 1998

A thrilling second-round encounter between England and Argentina was finely poised at 2-2 a couple of minutes into the second half when David Beckham was fouled by Diego Simeone. While still down on the turf, Beckham flicked his leg up catching Simeone lightly on the calf, but he went down as though he'd been run over by a tram. Referee Kim Nielsen applied the letter of the law and showed a red card to a distraught-looking Beckham. England went out on penalties and, back home, Beckham for a while became a national hate figure for his moment of madness. Simeone later admitted that his over-the-top reaction had helped get Beckham sent off – you don't say?

The Night it Rained Cards, 2006

In a second-round game between Portugal and the Netherlands in Nuremburg, Russian ref Valentin Ivanov made the classic error of setting the bar too low for his first booking. Although there were some tasty challenges and niggly fouls, this wasn't the dirtiest game ever.

Mark van Bommel: 'Next time, bring a box, shortarse.'

Here is the game expressed in FIFA stats:

Cautions: Mark van Bommel (Ne) 2 min, Khalid Boulahrouz (Ne) 7 min, Maniche (P) 20 min, Costinha (P) 31 min, Petit (P) 50 min, Giovanni van Bronckhorst (Ne) 59 min, Luis Figo (P) 60 min, Wesley Sneijder (Ne) 73 min, Deco (P) 73 min, Rafael van der Vaart (Ne) 74 min, Ricardo (P) 76 min, Nuno Valente (P) 76 min.
Sent off: Costinha (P) 45+1 min (2nd caution), Khalid Boulahrouz (Ne) 63 min (2nd caution), Deco (P) 78 min (2nd caution), Giovanni van Bronckhorst (Ne) 90+5 min (2nd caution).

Portugal won 1-0 thanks to a Maniche goal after 23 minutes, but a total of 16 cards were shown as the game ended up nine a side.

★ ★ ★

▦ INNOVATIONS

1934 ▪ Italy The first World Cup to require a qualifying process. Thirty-two nations entered the competition and 16 teams participated in the finals.

1938 ▪ France The first time that the hosts (France) and the title-holders (Italy) qualified automatically. Automatic qualification for the holders was rescinded in 2006.

1950 ▪ Brazil The first time the trophy was referred to as the Jules Rimet Cup. It was also the first (and last) time that there was no final match, but a final group of four.

1954 ▪ Switzerland The first time that teams were 'seeded', it was also the first tournament in which games were televised.

1970 ▪ Mexico Substitutes were used for the first time, with each side allowed two substitutions per game. This was also the first World Cup to be televised in colour. This tournament saw the introduction of yellow and red cards, used to indicate bookings and dismissals. These were the invention of English referee Ken Aston, inspired by traffic lights, who thought the game needed a system to make it clear when players had been cautioned.

1974 ▪ West Germany The first time the new World Cup trophy was presented to the winners. Number boards

'Listen Frannie, are you sure he hit him with that enormous piece of yellow cardboard?'

were first introduced to indicate the players involved in a substitution – another Ken Aston invention.

1986

■ Mexico For the first time, the last games of a group had to take place simultaneously, because of Austria and Germany's stitch-up of Algeria at Spain 1982.

1994

■ USA Due to the negativity of the 1990 World Cup, the system of three points for a win and one for a draw was initiated. Players' names appeared on the back of their shirts for the first time and motorised trolleys were employed to remove injured players from the field of play.

1998

■ France The Golden Goal was introduced, meaning that a team scoring in extra time was instantly declared the winner. It wasn't popular with players, referees, police or fans and has since been consigned to history.

▦ VITAL PUB INFO
TO FOSTER FRIENDLY RELATIONS WITH FANS OF

FRANCE

Fanspotter's guide

Tune into the Gauloise fug outside the boozer, where people are wearing *bleu* and waving their hands around as they talk.

Conversation starter

When the French national anthem, 'La Marseillaise' (think 'All You Need Is Love'), pipes up before the big opener against Uruguay, mention that its composer, artillery officer Rouget de l'Isle, fell asleep at his harpsichord and dreamed the words and music – the world's first crazy mixed-up hippy.

Accentuate the positive

Won the World Cup on home ground in 1998, and followed up with victory in Euro 2000.

'I Thierry Henry apologise to the Irish people for using my hand to knock them out of the World Cup finals'

Just in case anybody forgets how the French got to the finals. Bit of what goes around, comes around, anyone?

Skirt expertly around the negative

Slumped out in 2002 World Cup without a win, and their luck officially finally ran out in the 2006 World Cup final.

Form guide

Poor. Possibly deceptively so. Lost out to Serbia in their qualifying group, where they frequently struggled under coach Raymond Domenech. A highly dubious handball by skipper Thierry Henry carried them through the play-off against Ireland.

Four to watch

New world-class talent includes Karim Benzema and Lassana Diarra (both Real Madrid, the latter ex-Chelsea, Arsenal and Pompey), Hatem Ben Arfa (Marseille) and Samir Nasri (Arsenal).

Simply the best... ever

Zinédine 'Zizou' Zidane takes some beating for midfield *je ne sais quoi*; but we reckon he's edged by the great Michel Platini, who starred in the 1978, 82 and 86 finals.

Useful French phrases

Il s'écroule à l'entrée de la surface – He collapses on the edge of the area.

Ça frise l'incorrection – That verges on misconduct.

Chat-up line

Mademoiselle, could you please explain the difference between British kissing and French kissing?

This one's on me

A large crème de menthe, a double cognac and a cheeky little merlot, *s'il vous plait*.

Inside line on French culture

Doris: 'You have no values. Your whole life: it's nihilism, it's cynicism, it's sarcasm, and orgasm.'

Harry: 'You know, in France, I could run on that slogan and win.'

Woody Allen – *Deconstructing Harry* (1998)

Common ground

Booze cruises, Britain-bound refugee camps, *boeuf bourgignon* and Brigitte Bardot.

★ ★ ★

▦ SOUTH AMERICA V EUROPE

Ever since the World Cup began in 1930, no country from outside Europe or South America has ever won, but the balance of power has been constantly shifting since Uruguay took the first trophy (South American teams are listed first). No European team has ever won the World Cup outside of Europe.

■ 1930 – 1-0	Uruguay		■ 1974 – 5-5	West Germany
■ 1934 – 1-1	Italy		■ 1978 – 6-5	Argentina
■ 1938 – 1-2	Italy		■ 1982 – 6-6	Italy
■ 1950 – 2-2	Uruguay		■ 1986 – 7-6	Argentina
■ 1954 – 2-3	West Germany		■ 1990 – 7-7	West Germany
■ 1958 – 3-3	Brazil		■ 1994 – 8-7	Brazil
■ 1962 – 4-3	Brazil		■ 1998 – 8-8	France
■ 1966 – 4-4	England		■ 2002 – 9-8	Brazil
■ 1970 – 5-4	Brazil		■ 2006 – 9-9	Italy

⠿ EBAY WORLD CUP

SOLD

£417.00 • Panini 74 World Cup Munich 1974 383/400 Stickers • Rare
Hmm, we're still glad our mums chucked ours out in the big spring clean of 1987.

£80.00 • World Cup Medal Brazil 1950
A megabargain on eBay from September 2007 – a genuine World Cup winner's medal from the first post-war tournament, sold for a song by a seller in Uruguay.

£11.01 • Mint Set of 1966 England World Cup Stamps
4d, 6d, 1/3d and the 4d again overprinted with 'England Winners' [bought by myself] – plus a First Day Cover issued at Harrow and Wembley Post Office.

As designed by somebody who has never seen a football match. The only vague likeness is Gordon Banks on the 1/3 stamp (whatever that means), who appears to be playing for either Sheffield Wednesday or Barnsley during the 1966 World Cup.

£1.04 • World Cup Spain 1982 Vintage leather belt 44ins
One of the few World Cup collectables guaranteed to keep your trousers up.

£0.99 • Trivial Pursuit World Cup France 1998 Official Edition
Why?

★ ★ ★

⠿ KITASTROPHES

1974 Netherlands

The Dutch FA had a deal with adidas to supply their kit – with the three stripes on the shirtsleeves – for the 1974 World Cup in West Germany, but Netherlands' superstar Johan Cruyff was having none of it. He already had a personal deal with Puma and refused to wear kit endorsed by a rival firm. The KNVB gave in to Cruyff's demands, and he had a specially made kit with just two stripes on the sleeves, shorts and socks.

'Ooh! Hark at Mister Two Stripes!' Johan Cruyff pictured shortly after having a fag and losing the World Cup final.

Four years on, Cruyff decided not to go to the 1978 World Cup for personal reasons, but his awkward spirit lived on: twins Rene and Willy van de Kerkhof both insisted on a 33.3 percent reduction on the adidas norm. Apparently this ingrained trait of non-conformism can be traced back to the Middle Age bourgeois Dutch traders who developed a keen sense of independence and individualism, and a deep distrust of authority.

1974 Scotland

During the tournament in West Germany, members of the Scotland squad fell out with their boot manufacturers over bonus payments and diligently blacked out all of their brand marks with black boot polish.

1978 France

France and Hungary both walked out of the tunnel wearing white shirts for their Group One game at Mar del Plata. Although Hungary's red and

France's blue did not clash, Argentinian TV was only broadcasting in black and white and so one team had to wear white, though both teams seem to have got that message. The kick-off was delayed for half an hour while a new strip was frantically sought, and it was local side Club Atletico Kimberley who came to the rescue, supplying a set of their basic cotton green and white striped shirts, which were worn by France. Kimberley's rather snug-fitting shirts served the French well, with them beating Hungary 3-1.

1994 Mexico

Eccentric goalkeeper Jorge Campos was allowed to design his own outfits, and came up with some outrageous geometric, day-glo creations that defy accurate description. One had zig-zags and rectangles on it, mainly involving a violent orange, steward jacket yellow, fuchsia pink, acid lime green, black, white and so on. So distracting was this garish strip that it could almost qualify as being an unfair advantage, should a striker find himself one-on-one with Campos.

1994 Cameroon

For the USA World Cup, Cameroon and UK kit makers Mitre planned a daring new design based on the national flag. Sadly there was an oversight at Fédération Camerounaise de Football and their three-panelled green, red and gold strip, with a large gold star in the middle, had to be binned. FIFA had not received the kit registration papers by the deadline and told the Indomitable Lions that they had to play in a comparatively disappointing plain green with red shorts and yellow socks.

2002 Cameroon

More kit trouble for Cameroon, who wore basketball-style sleeveless shirts made by Puma for their triumphant campaign in the 2002 African Cup of Nations in Mali. FIFA didn't approve and told Cameroon they could not be worn in the 2002 South Korea/Japan World Cup. Puma produced the same design, but with black sleeves, for the tournament.

Ever the innovators, Cameroon went on to sport a figure-hugging one-piece kit for the group stages of the 2004 African Cup of Nations in Tunisia. During that tournament, FIFA told Cameroon that the strip was against equipment regulations and they could not wear it for the knockout stages. Puma claimed they couldn't supply new strip in time and so Cameroon defied the order and wore their 'UniQT' for a quarter-final meeting with Nigeria. FIFA reacted with an £85,000 fine for the Cameroon FA and a six-point deduction for their World Cup qualifying campaign, though the

points were later restored by FIFA's general assembly. Puma, who claimed that the strip had been approved by people within FIFA, sued the sport's governing body. An out-of-court settlement was reached 'in the interests of international football'.

Having won the 2002 African Cup of Nations, the Cameroon players celebrate the news that their sleeves would now be returned.

★ ★ ★

▦ VITAL PUB INFO
TO FOSTER FRIENDLY RELATIONS WITH FANS OF

ARGENTINA

Fanspotter's guide
Look out for the white and sky-blue shirts of the Albicelestes (which means white and sky-blue, incidentally – think 'albino' white; think 'celestial' blue).

Conversation starter
Is Diego Maradona really the man for the job of Argentine coach? Even in triumph at qualification, Maradona told his doubters to 'suck it and keep sucking it', earning a FIFA fine and ban.

Accentuate the positive

In Italia 90, only the hosts prevented Argentina lifting their third World Cup in four finals.

Skirt expertly around the negative

And that was the last time they even made the semis.

Form guide

Finished on a high in South American qualifying, with vital wins against Peru and a last-gasp clincher against Uruguay. Before that, however, they slumped under soon-to-be ex-coach Coco Basile, registering losses against Colombia, Chile (the first in 35 years), Bolivia (6-1!), Ecuador, Brazil and Paraguay.

One to watch

Barcelona winger/playmaker/wizard of dribble Lionel Messi is the reigning World and European Player of the Year, having been second in the world for the past two years. He made his Barça debut at 16, has won three La Liga titles, two European Cups and a Spanish Cup, not forgetting the Under-20 World Cup and 2008 Olympic gold with Argentina. And he's still only 22.

Simply the best... ever

It's got to be that man Maradona.

Diego adamantly denied rumours that he was stuck in a rut.

Useful Spanish phrases

Mano, signor arbitro! – Handball, referee!

Que sayer grande, tengo que ahogar mis penas – Make it a large one, I'm drowning my sorrows (useful for when England/Argentina knocks out Argentina/England).

Chat-up line

Serenade her with 'Don't Cry For Me Argentina', taking care to burst into tears with the line 'I love you and hope you love me'.

This one's on me

Corned beef hash, with side orders of steak and Desperate Dan meat pie.

Inside line on Argentine culture

Eat more beef per capita than any other nation.

Common ground

First there was World Cup '78 full-back Alberto Tarantini (Birmingham City), closely followed by the legendary Ossie Ardiles and Ricky Villa (Spurs). Man Utd and Chelsea flop Juan Veron, now 35, was a huge midfield presence who steered his country through the qualifiers, abetted by Carlos Tevez (Man City) and Javier Mascherano (Liverpool).

★ ★ ★

▦ TALKING A GOOD GAME

I told him he was whistling for the Italians and he would have done better to have put on a blue shirt from the beginning and swallowed his whistle. He should have sent me off; the fact he didn't shows that he had no authority.

West Germany's Uli Stielike, after the 1982 World Cup final

▦ WORLD CUP SONGS
WEST GERMANY 1974

England World Cup Squad with Magnum Brass • 'Here We Are'
(Failed to chart)
A nasty tiddly-om-pom-pom military band drowns out a grudging squad
performance: 'England's having a ball / What a day for one and all', my arse.
This supposedly perky cack's failure to dent the charts wasn't entirely down to
the team's flop in the qualifiers. How did this record ever get the go-ahead
to be made? Even now, the misplaced optimism still has the power to wound.

Meanwhile, the Scotland World Cup Squad's 1974 effort was 'Easy
Easy', a lumpen party piece notable only for the audacious rhyming of
'Yabadabadoo' with 'We are the boys in blue'.

ARGENTINA 1978

Andy Cameron • 'Ally's Tartan Army'
(Number 6)
With England tragically absent again, it was up to Scotland to carry at least
part of the Union Jack into battle – and the Lions were at least mentioned in
dispatches: Andy Cameron's 'Ally's Tartan Army' swaggered famously about
'the greatest fitba team's' impending victory, and stuck the boot in quite
magnificently with the pay-off line: 'We're representing Britain / And we're
gaunny do or die / England cannae dae it / 'Cos they didnae qualify.' Mind
you, we didn't lose to Iran, either.

At least London-born-and-raised, thoroughly English Rod Stewart
(featuring the Scottish World Cup Squad) clawed back a bit of pride for
England by pipping Andy Cameron (number 6 in April) with 'Ole Ola
(Mulher Brasileira)', hitting number 4 in June.

★ ★ ★

▦ WHAT THE PAPERS SAY
1966 WORLD CUP

When the World Cup came to England, the organisers knew that what it
was really about was royalty. The Official Souvenir Programme (price 2/6)
outlined how the opening ceremony would unfold:

THE OPENING CEREMONY

■ **6 p.m.**

Programme of Music by the Massed Bands of the Grenadier Guards, the Coldstream Guards, and the Irish Guards.

■ **6.40 p.m**

Marching Display by the Massed Bands of the Brigade of Guards: the Grenadier Guards, Coldstream Guards, Irish Guards, Scots Guards, and the Welsh Guards.

■ **7.05 p.m.**

Flag bearing ceremony of the competing nations.

■ **7.15 p.m.**

Her Majesty the Queen accompanied by His Royal Highness, The Duke of Edinburgh, arrives on the arena.

■ Fanfare of Trumpets.

■ National Anthem.

■ Her Majesty is invited by Sir Stanley Rous, President of F.I.F.A., to open the Final Series of the Eighth World Championship.

■ Her Majesty declares the Championship open.

■ Raising of flags of competing nations.

■ Teams enter the arena.

■ Presentation of Officials to Her Majesty.

■ Uruguayan National Anthem.

■ Teams presented to Her Majesty.

■ **7.30 p.m.**

KICK-OFF. ENGLAND V URUGUAY

Typically shabby French trick. We give the game to the world and then they try to invent a World Cup with a French name on the end of it. Jules Rimet, my arse. Funny how they weren't so keen to stick their name on any of the World Wars in which they ended up waiting for us to bail them out.

★ ★ ★

▦ FIFTH PLACE PLAQUE ALERT!
SLIGHTLY CRAP FIFA WORLD CUP REGULATIONS

▦ **Article 1.5** The associations that take part in the final competition will each be awarded a souvenir plaque.

▦ **1.6** The associations ranked first, second, third and fourth in the final competition will each receive a diploma.

▦ **1.7** 45 medals will be presented to each of the three top teams in the final competition. No further medals will be awarded.

▦ **1.8** The team ranked fourth will receive an award.

▦ **1.9** The referees, assistant referees, fourth and fifth officials at the play-off for third place and final match will each receive an award.

★ ★ ★

▦ VITAL PUB INFO
TO FOSTER FRIENDLY RELATIONS WITH FANS OF

NIGERIA

Fanspotter's guide

Home in on the green-shirted bongo party.

Conversation starter

Tch. That blinkin' Maradona, eh? (Former dictator Ibrahim Babangida is known as 'Maradona' for the way he cheated Nigeria's citizens in the 1980s and 90s, wriggling out of tricky media questions.)

Accentuate the positive

Back in 1994, Nigeria were one minute away from beating Italy and going into the quarter-finals.

Skirt expertly around the negative

That remains their all-time high point, except for upsetting Spain in 1998.

Form guide

A near miracle provided qualification, as Nigeria came back from 1-0 down at half time against Kenya, while group leaders Algeria almost spookily stumbled against Mozambique. And miracles don't happen twice. Nigeria finished third in the 2010 African Cup of Nations, beating Algeria in the play-off.

One to watch

It's got to be Portsmouth's Nwankwo Kanu, but Wolfsburg striker Obafemi Martins can blow just as hot and/or cold.

Simply the best... ever

Rashidi Yekini scored a record 37 goals in 70 international starts, and scored the Super Eagles' first ever goal at the World Cup finals in 1994.

Useful Nigerian Pidgin English phrases

Dat gel get chop wowo lick plate – The girl has been hit by the ugly stick.

You no sabi di tin wey we dey tok – You cannot understand what we are talking about.

Chat-up line

I once sent £200 to a Nigerian prince who was down on his luck and promised to repay me once he'd claimed his rightful inheritance of £50 million. I guess he sent you?

This one's on me

At 7.5 percent, Nigerian Guinness is far stronger than the Irish stuff. It's bitter and malty-tasting, available in off licences throughout South London.

Inside line on Nigerian culture

Nigerians live in a fast-growing economy with lucrative gas and oil reserves. Remember how that used to feel?

Common ground

Back in the 1980s, African soccer trailblazers John Chiedozie and Tunji Banjo lit up the Third Division with Orient.

★ ★ ★

▦ TALKING A GOOD GAME

I'm sure that some of those in the stands are faintly amused to see a child on the field in a World Cup match.

Pelé, on his World Cup debut, aged 17

▦ NICE NAMES

- Jim Gentle (USA, 1930)
- Jorge Pardon (Peru, 1930)
- Roger Bocquet (Switzerland, 1950)
- Adolphe Hug (Switzerland, 1950)
- Lazlo Kiss (Hungary, 1982)
(Did Lazlo Kiss ever meet Adolphe Hug?)
- Mustafa Merry (Morocco, 1986)
- Brian Bliss (USA, 1990)

- Hakan Mild (Sweden, 1994)
- Roy Keane (Republic of Ireland, 1994, 1998, 2002)
- Phillipe Clement (Belgium, 1998)
- Tim Flowers (England, 1998)
- William Sun Sing (Costa Rica, 2002)
- Omar Bravo (Mexico, 2006)
- Love (Angola, 2006)

★ ★ ★

▦ WHATEVER HAPPENED TO THE HEROES?

Tore André Flo • Norway 1998

The hero of what was arguably Norway's greatest game in the finals, when they came from behind to beat Brazil in 1998 – the lanky dangerman scoring the equaliser then getting tripped for the deciding last-minute penalty. From the heights (6'4") of playing 76 times for his country, and winning the FA, Cup-Winners' and League Cups with Chelsea, he then downsized with Rangers – and so to Sunderland, and lowly Leeds. In 2009, there was an inauspicious career end for 'Flonaldo': coaxed into a comeback by old Chelsea mukka Bob Di Matteo, Flo started just two games for MK Dons. Then he fluffed the vital shootout penalty in the third-tier play-offs. Then he was released.

Hakan Sükür • Turkey 2002

The man who scored the fastest-ever goal at any World Cup finals – hitting the net against South Korea in 10.8 seconds – 'The Bull of the Bosphorus' is the greatest Turkish goalscorer of all time, with 264 league goals in 533 appearances worldwide. He's such a legend in Turkey, his wedding was televised live in 2002 – the year his goals claimed World Cup third place for his country. Best remembered for three trophy-heavy spells with Galatasaray between 1992 and his retirement in 2008, he made somewhat less of a mark during short stops at Torino, Inter, Parma and Blackburn Rovers. He's now a commentator with the Turkish Radio and Television Corporation, but has his badges and says he wants to become a coach.

Jorge Valdano • Argentina
1982, 1986

Valdano was not only responsible for the iffy through-ball that led to the 'Hand of God' goal, but he also scored a goal in the final, lifting the World Cup with Argentina. He coached Real Madrid to the Spanish title in 1994 – and currently basks in the role of president of the Spanish giants. But, above all, he's a football philosopher and the editor of two books. 'Football is an excuse to make us happy,' he has opined. And yet 'Football is a fiesta of identity and a secular religion, in danger of dying of seriousness.' He doesn't like the 'ugly' football played by British teams. He lives for the beauty of the game, for moments of poetry which can be lost in merely 'efficient' football, paraphrasing Argentinian poet Jorge Luis Borges: 'What is a sunrise for? What are caresses for? What is the smell of coffee for? They are for pleasure, for emotion, for living.'

It was the largest business card most of the delegates had ever seen.

★ ★ ★

⠿ BAD HAIR XI

1 David Seaman • England, 2002 'Safe Hands' was sporting the classic 'Englishman in a mid-life crisis' ponytail. Did he go to games in a red Triumph Stag?

2 Dan Petrescu • Romania, 1998 After Romania beat England in France, the Chelsea defender dyed his hair blond. This wouldn't have been much of a deal except that the entire Romanian team had also reached for the bleach... a commentator's nightmare.

Forget the hair, check the shirt tucking-in thing – it's still fashionable in certain parts of North Wales.

3 Christian Ziege • Germany, 2002 Appeared in the Japan/South Korea tournament sporting a full-on Mohawk... not a pretty sight.

4 Alexi Lalas • USA, 1994 A combination of rock festival hair and huge goatee beard in Viking red made Lalas look more like someone who had taken a wrong turn from the late 1960s, rather than a '90s footballer.

5 Taribo West • Nigeria, 2002 Never one to be predictable, Taribo showed up for Japan/South Korea wearing little green horns.

6 Rudi Voeller • West Germany, 1990 Classic grey German footballer's perm – even some of Frank Rijkaard's 'special gel' couldn't rescue it.

7 Carlos Valderrama • Colombia, 1990. More hair than anyone has a right to own.

8 Roberto Baggio • Italy, 1994 The Divine Ponytail... The missed penalty... Coincidence? We think not.

9 Peter Beardsley • England, 1986 Every schoolboy in the mid-1970s had this pudding bowl template style, but Peter kept it.

10 Ronaldo • Brazil, 2002 A unique variation on the classic number one all over – leaving a strange semi-circle shape at the front. Ridiculous?

11 Chris Waddle • England, 1990 An early exponent of the classic footballer's hair-don't – the spiky on top, short at the sides, long down the back 'Mullet'.

▦ VITAL PUB INFO

TO FOSTER FRIENDLY RELATIONS WITH FANS OF

SOUTH KOREA

Fanspotter's guide

Clue: the team's nickname is the 'Red Devils'. Man U's Park Ji-Sung won't have to change his kit or nickname.

Conversation starter

Blimey, it's eight World Cups on the trot for the Korean Republic.

Accentuate the positive

Reached the semi-finals in 2002, the first Asian team ever to do so.

Skirt expertly around the negative

To be fair, that was on home soil – and there were rumours of match-fixing and refs in the pocket as they kicked their way into the record books.

Form guide

The best Asian team by a long chalk in qualifying, but perhaps better assessed by more recent friendlies where they beat Senegal, drew with Denmark and lost to Serbia in front of 6,500 fans at Fulham's Craven Cottage!

One to watch

FC Seoul midfielder Ki Sung-Yeung has recently signed for Celtic, having won AFC Young Player of the Year.

Simply the best... ever

Cha Bum-Kun – 121 caps (55 goals) between 1972 and 1986, winning the 1988 UEFA Cup with Bayer Leverkusen. Then on to K-League management, taking charge of the national side at France 98.

Useful Korean phrases

...... – Bless you! (According to Korean etiquette, it's the height of bad manners to acknowledge the fact that someone just sneezed.)

Ku-got han-gung-mal-lo mwo-ra-go hae-yo? – What's that called in Korean? (Useful in avoiding etiquette problems if the Korean team are flukey, filthy or cheaty.)

Chat-up line

As the old Korean proverb says, 'A turtle only travels when it sticks its neck out.'

This one's on me

South Korea's three top domestic beers are brewed using rice. A pint of cooking lager and a saki chaser might do the trick.

Inside line on South Korean culture

The taegukki flag features a sideways '69' symbol representing yin and yang, or balance and harmony. The four kwae symbols surrounding it can stand for the four elements, the four compass points or the four seasons (backing up Frankie Valli).

Common ground

A Tale of Two Sisters is a dead scary cult horror movie from Kim Ji-woon. Not giving anything away plotwise, there seems to be a deformed girl, apparently painted with tar, lurking under the kitchen sink.

★ ★ ★

WHAT IF…?

■ The finals had started up again in 1949 after the war, as FIFA intended? Would England have won the World Cup in 1965? And would we now all be able to go down the bookies and have a large winning punt because the finals would already have been played in 2009?

■ The attempted name-change to 'World's Cup' had caught on in 1934?

■ Nigeria hadn't been disqualified from the 1974 World Cup finals because of crowd trouble experienced during a qualifier against Ghana. If that match hadn't been abandoned, who's to say Nigeria wouldn't have made a difference?

■ Manchester United manager Matt Busby hadn't been injured in the Munich air disaster on 6 February 1958, and had taken up his appointment as Scotland manager for the Sweden World Cup that year? Surely then they might not have bombed out bottom of their group with just one point from matches against France, Paraguay and Yugoslavia?

■ And what if Wales boss and Manchester United assistant manager Jimmy Murphy had been on the ill-fated flight in Munich, instead of attending a Welsh World Cup qualifying match? As things turned out, Wales reached the quarter-finals and narrowly lost to Brazil, flying the flag for the home nations along with Northern Ireland, while England joined Scotland on the first ferry home.

■ Munich hadn't happened, and England had played the 1958 World Cup with Roger Byrne (33 caps), Tommy Taylor (19), Duncan Edwards (18) and David Pegg (1)? Don't forget, in the run-up to the World Cup, England beat

Brazil 4-2, France (third place) 2-0 at Wembley, and West Germany (fourth place) 3-1 in Berlin.

■ England had taken up FIFA's offer of a place in the France 1938 finals, after Austria withdrew following the German invasion? We did, after all, travel to France that year and beat the hosts in a friendly in Paris. England also beat a FIFA XI 3-0 at Highbury, Germany 6-3 in Berlin and Norway 4-0 at St James' Park.

■ Scotland had taken part in 1938? They beat Hungary, the eventual runners-up, 3-1 in Glasgow.

■ Jimmy Greaves had claimed his 'rightful' place as centre-forward in 1966, overriding Alf Ramsey's decision to stick with a winning side?

■ Maradona had been spotted by the ref, and booked for deliberate handball?

One of the least memorable World Cup goals ever scored.

▦ TURNCOATS

■ Argentinian Luis Monti scored for his country in the 1930 World Cup, but switched sides to play for Italy in 1934 – and this time earned a winner's medal!

■ Raimundo Orsi was another Argentinian turncoat. After winning 13 caps for Argentina (scoring 3 goals), he swiftly followed this by making 35 appearances for Italy (13 goals) and also picked up a World Cup winner's medal in 1934.

■ And Enrique Guaita was yet another to make the same move! Hmm, maybe it's no surprise Argentina were knocked out in the first round in 1934. But it was quite a turn-up for the books when Argentina allowed Guaita to switch back again in 1937!

■ Alfredo di Stefano, cited by some as the finest footballer who ever lived, played first for his native Argentina, then Colombia and finally Spain – but nevertheless he had an uncanny knack of missing World Cup finals.

■ 1958 World Cup final star Mazzola of Brazil switched nationality for the 1962 World Cup – appearing for Italy under the name on his passport, José Altafini.

★ ★ ★

▦ THE FATE OF WORLD CUP FREEBIES ON EBAY

£49.99 • adidas Referee Box Set From 2002 World Cup Korea FIFA
'Rare case given to tournament referees' (and obviously not exactly treasured by the ungrateful sods).

£49.99 • World Cup 98, England footballer mobile phone AUTHENTIC
Offered for sale on eBay in 2004 (minus SIM card, by the way!). 'One of the original One 2 One phones given to each England squad member for their personal use. Thought to have been used by Sol Campbell during the championships, this is a one-off piece of memorabilia which is unlikely to be found again anywhere else.' Went unsold.

£10.00 • Esso 1970 World Cup Coin Collection • 1 Missing Coin
Ah yes, the cardboard display case, the slightly dodgy way the coins slipped into their holes... ensuring there was always one missing coin!

£6.99 • 1966 World Cup Beer Mat, Ansells, Birmingham • Rare

A 'Welcome/Willkommen/Bienvenido' jobbie designed to welcome world visitors to Brum for Villa Park matches... and sadly nicked by a Brummie, instead.

£0.99 • ITV World Cup Brochure For 1978

'Join ITV and Ally's Army for World Cup '78,' it says here. There are '62 pages full of articles and pictures in colour as well as b/w. Special section on Scotland. Match report section untouched.'

£0.99 • Sunday People 1992 Double-Sided World Cup Poster

Shame there wasn't a World Cup in 1992! On closer inspection, it turns out to be from 2002: 'Double Sided, Approx Size 590mm x 410mm. May Suite [sic] Collector. Used Condition – No Writing.' Eh?

£0.01 • FIFA World Cup 2006 City Guide • Cologne/Koln

'Official fold-out leaflet in English offering a brief guide to the World Cup hosting city of Cologne. In perfect condition.'

In many circles – well, beer mat collecting circles – this is worth a fortune. I'd no idea either, but it was a nice gesture from the good burghers of Birmingham. It has a reserve price of £17 on a certain internet auction site.

★ ★ ★

▦ TALKING A GOOD GAME

Pelé after Gordon Banks' wonder save, Brazil v England, 1970

At that moment I hated Gordon Banks more than any man in soccer. But when I cooled down I had to applaud him with my heart for the greatest save I had ever seen.

▦ VITAL PUB INFO
TO FOSTER FRIENDLY RELATIONS WITH FANS OF

GREECE

Fanspotter's guide

If you notice a blue shirt cunningly self-coloured with a cross and some stripes, so as to resemble a chunk of flag, then its wearer will most likely be Greek.

Conversation starter

Mamma Mia! knocked the spots off *My Big Fat Greek Wedding* – which in turn eclipsed the Euromantic charm of *Shirley Valentine*.

Accentuate the positive

Won the Euros in 2004, beating hosts Portugal in the opening game and again in the final.

Skirt expertly around the negative

That first match in 2004 was their first win in any major tournament. Ever. (They lost all three games at the US 1994 finals.)

Form guide

A qualifying group featuring Israel, Switzerland, Moldova, Latvia and Luxembourg was hardly a Group of Death, but Greece still needed to come through the play-offs, finally beating Ukraine.

One to watch

Nuremberg striker Angelos Charisteas is most likely to score Greece's first-ever goal in the World Cup finals.

Simply the best... ever

In the 1980s, long-haired maverick Vassilis Hatzipanagis was dubbed 'The Footballing Nureyev' for his dazzling dribbling skills. He only ever played one game for Greece due to eligibility problems, having played for the Russian Under-21s.

Useful Greek phrases

Deep-sao – I'm thirsty.

O kírios tha plirosi gia ola – This gentleman will pay for everything.

Chat-up line

Pinch my Elgin Marbles, baby.

This one's on me

Ouzo goes cloudy in water, tastes like aniseed, and makes you fall over.

Inside line on Greek culture

Some 2400 years ago, Socrates, Aristotle and Plato laid the foundations of Western philosophy. But only one of them was good enough to make the Brazilian World Cup team.

Common ground

Greece's most-capped player and Euro-lifting legend, Theo Zagorakis, is still remembered fondly by Leicester fans. He played for the Foxes for three seasons at the end of the 1990s.

★ ★ ★

▦ ONE-TOURNAMENT WONDERS

Of this year's 32 competitors, only Slovakia are making their World Cup debut, compared with seven nations in 2006. North Korea have had to wait longest for a second appearance (since 1966, when they became the first Asian side to make the second phase after they famously beat Italy at Ayresome Park in Middlesbrough and then went 3-0 up against Portugal in the quarter-finals, before Eusebio inspired a spectacular comeback). Honduras and New Zealand (1982), Greece (1994), Slovenia (2002), Ghana and Ivory Coast (2006) are all due to make a second appearance in the finals this summer.

Cuba (1938)

The Cubans got off to a cracking start beating Romania 2-1 in a first round replay, but then ran into a yellow wall in the second round when Sweden beat them 8-0. A reporter at the game commented: 'Up to five goals is journalism, after that it is statistics.'

Dutch East Indies (1938)

The country now known as Indonesia lost 6-0 to Hungary in their only World Cup game to date: a 14,000-mile round trip to France, for one heavy defeat, possibly representing the most effort for least return in the history of the game.

Wales (1958)

One of the best-ever Welsh sides were runners-up to Czechoslovakia in qualifying Group 4, missing out on qualification to the World Cup in Sweden. But the troubled situation in the Middle East had a happy outcome for the Red Dragons when Egypt and Sudan refused to play Israel in their qualifying group, while Indonesia would consider meeting them only on neutral territory. FIFA therefore declared Israel winners of their group but decided they must play one of the European runners-up if they were to go to Sweden. Belgium were drawn out of a hat, but didn't fancy the fixture. Wales were next and so faced Israel in a two-legged play-off. The Welsh won 2-0 in Tel Aviv and repeated the scoreline at Ninian Park.

It was a circuitous route to Sweden, but Wales acquitted themselves well, drawing with Hungary, Mexico and Sweden. Three points earned them a play-off with Hungary, which they won 2-1 thanks to goals from Ivor Allchurch and Terry Medwin. In the quarter-finals, Wales met Brazil in Gothenburg, but a young 17-year-old by the name of Pelé scored the only goal of the game and Wales' only World Cup adventure was over. Many in Wales still feel the result could have been different that day had John Charles not been injured for the fixture.

Israel (1970)

The troubled political situation in the Middle East has led to Israel competing in Asia, Europe and Oceania World Cup qualifiers before they

Nobody won the spot-the-ball competition that week as Wales beat Hungary in their play-off. And that includes the seven people in the stands and not actually playing. Okay, forget the ref.

finally became full members of UEFA in 1994. Their solitary World Cup appearance was in 1970 when they lost 2-0 to Uruguay, drew 1-1 with Sweden and managed a 0-0 shut-out against eventual finalists Italy.

Haiti (1974)

The Caribbean island was in the grip of the horrific regime of 'Baby Doc' Duvalier, who decided that Haiti were going to qualify for a World Cup, come what may. The qualifying CONCACAF Championship was held entirely in Haiti and many refereeing decisions mysteriously went their way.

Haiti's World Cup started rather well when Emmanuel Sanon put them 1-0 up against Italy in the Olympiastadion, Munich. However, Italy pulled things round and managed a 3-1 victory. The day after the game, defender Ernst Jean-Joseph tested positive in a dope test and was manhandled back to the training camp and beaten up by Haitian officials before being sent home.

The next game, in the same spectacular surroundings, went less well with England's conquerors Poland dismantling Haiti to the tune of 7-0; and they were then convincingly beaten 4-1 by Argentina. The Duvalier regime was overthrown in 1986, and Haiti haven't made it to a World Cup since.

East Germany (1974)

The Deutsche Demokratische Republik national football side was in existence from 1952 when full FIFA membership was attained until German reunification in 1990. They achieved little in those 38 years, remaining in the shadow of neighbours West Germany, except for the one meeting between the two sides, which occurred in the 1974 World Cup. Both sides had already qualified for the next round, but this was a politically sensitive fixture. Jürgen Sparwasser, who scored the only goal in this clash of ideologies as East beat West, claimed: 'According to the rumours, I was richly rewarded for the goal, with a car, a house and a cash premium. But that is not true.'

Although the players all received the Meister des Sports award for their triumph over Capitalism, they would have been much better off losing because victory landed them in a second round group with Brazil, Argentina and Holland. West Germany may have lost the 'German derby', but they went on to win the World Cup.

Zaire (1974)

Now known as the Democratic Republic of the Congo, Zaire went to West Germany as newly crowned African Champions in 1974. The Leopards failed to make much of an impression, however. They played reasonably well in a 2-0 defeat to Scotland, but were then thrashed 9-0 by Yugoslavia in

Mwanza Mukombo goes in foot high on Luis Pereira in Zaire's 3-0 defeat to Brazil.

Gelsenkirchen. Brazil then beat them 3-0 in the last group game. For many the abiding memory of Zaire's World Cup came from the Brazil game when the champions were awarded a free-kick 25 yards out. On hearing the referee's whistle, right-back Mwepu Ilunga charged out of the Zaire wall and hoofed the ball upfield, looking rather hurt when he received a yellow card.

Behind the humour, however, a more sinister story has since emerged. Ilunga has claimed that Zairean Football Federation officials pilfered their wages, and they learnt just before the Yugoslavia game that they would make no financial gain from the tournament. 'Before the Yugoslavia match we learnt that we were not going to be paid, so we refused to play.' The side were talked into playing the game, but the fact that they were 6-0 down by half time illustrates that their hearts were no longer in it.

Zaire's leader Mobutu Sese Seko decided that a pep talk was in order and sent his presidential guards round to the team hotel. According to Ilunga: 'They closed the hotel to all journalists and said that if we lost 0-4 to Brazil, none of us would be able to return home.' A 3-0 scoreline suited Brazil, because it edged out Scotland on goal difference, and Zaire, who understandably wanted to go home to their families... 3-0 it was.

Kuwait (1982)

Kuwait's Spanish adventure began well, with a 1-1 draw against Czechoslovakia, but soon descended into farce when they met France in Valladolid. France went 3-0 up with goals from Bernard Genghini, Michel Platini and Didier Six, before Abdullah Al-Balushi pulled one back from a quickly taken free-kick. Alain Giresse appeared to have extinguished any hopes of a comeback when he netted to put France 4-1 ahead, but the Kuwaitis surrounded Soviet referee Miroslav Stupar, protesting that they had stopped playing when they heard a whistle, which had come from the crowd.

The ref was unmoved and it appeared that Kuwait were going to leave the field when the stately figure of Sheikh Fahid Al-Ahmad Al-Sabah, president of the Kuwaiti Football Association and brother of the Kuwaiti Emir, made his way from his seat in the Royal Box down to the pitch. After a bit of a ticking off from the Sheikh, Stupar performed a spectacular u-turn and disallowed the goal. The French were rather miffed at this (it was the fourth French goal that the ref had disallowed), but Maxime Bossis soon restored the three-goal advantage, sneaking one in at the near post.

Canada (1986)

For a large country with around 33 million people, many of them of British extraction, you have to wonder why Canada aren't a bit better at football. The Canucks' solitary World Cup appearance came in Mexico in 1986 where they lost 1-0 to France, 2-0 to Hungary and 2-0 to the USSR, flying home goalless and pointless.

Iraq (1986)

It is a wonder that Iraq have ever managed to qualify for a World Cup. The only time they achieved it, in 1986, they had to play all their home games on neutral territory due to the Iran-Iraq War. Since then the Lions of Mesopotamia have had to contend with far worse. Saddam Hussein's pathological son Uday was placed in charge of the national side for the 1994 and 1998 qualifying campaigns, and he employed torture and imprisonment of players as a motivational tool. Own goals or missed penalties were punished with brutal floggings and prison sentences.

In Mexico, Iraq lost 1-0 to Paraguay and 2-1 to Belgium, with the nation's greatest ever player Ahmed Radhi scoring their goal. They also lost their third game, against hosts Mexico, 1-0, but at least they got to play in front of over 103,000 at the Azteca Stadium.

United Arab Emirates (1990)

Italia 90 was only the UAE's second attempt at qualifying for a World Cup, and the Falcons went unbeaten against Syria, North Yemen, South Korea, Qatar, China, Saudi Arabia and North Korea to get there. However, in Group D in Italia 90 they lost 2-0 to Colombia, 5-1 to West Germany and 4-1 to Yugoslavia, despite the not inconsiderable incentive of a Ferrari Testarossa for each player if they made it to the second round.

Jamaica's Ricardo Gardener dances through a late Japanese challenge on the way to their only win in the World Cup finals.

Jamaica (1998)

Jamaica has a patchy history of attempting to qualify for the World Cup. They first attempted it in 1966 and got to the final qualifying round, but were out of their depth losing 8-0 to Mexico and 7-0 to Costa Rica. In the 1970 qualifiers, they had taken a step backwards, with a 100 percent record of defeats. For 1974 they had to suspend 17 players for poor behaviour on a trip to Bermuda and in 1978 they lost out to Cuba, while in 1982 they couldn't afford the entrance fee, and in 1986 they were suspended for financial reasons.

They finally made it in 1998, playing their first World Cup game against Croatia in Lens. Although Robbie Earle levelled after the Croatians took the lead, the Reggae Boyz lost 3-1. They then lost 5-0 against Argentina in Paris, but made the trip worthwhile with a 2-1 win over Japan in Lyon thanks to a brace from Theodore Whitmore.

Senegal (2002)

Senegal caused a sensation in their first-ever appearance in the World Cup finals, beating the holders and European Champions France in the opening game of the 2002 tournament. The Lions of Teranga beat their former colonial masters, with Bouba Diop scoring the only goal of the game after half an hour. France never recovered, flying home after the group stage with a single point to their name, while Senegal drew 1-1 with Denmark and 3-3 with Uruguay to qualify for the knockout stages.

They continued to confound expectations, beating Sweden 2-1 after extra time, having trailed to a Henrik Larsson goal, with Henri Camara scoring twice. In the quarter-finals the West Africans held out until the seventh minute of extra time against Turkey when a goal from Ilhan Mansiz finally sent them home.

China (2002)

China withdrew from FIFA between 1958 and 1979, and had several close calls in the following years, most notably a defeat to Hong Kong in Beijing when they needed only a draw to qualify for Mexico 86. With the region's strongest sides, Japan and South Korea, qualifying as joint-hosts, the way opened up for China to qualify at last. Indonesia, Maldives and Cambodia were swept aside in the initial group stage, and then China came top of a group containing United Arab Emirates, Uzbekistan, Qatar and Oman. Like many who had gone before them, China found the real thing to be rather more difficult than the qualifiers. They lost 2-0 to Costa Rica; 4-0 to Brazil and 3-0 to Turkey. At least they didn't have far to go home.

Germany World Cup (2006)

The increasingly less exclusive 'One-Tournament Wonders' club was rather wrecked in 2006 when Angola, Togo, Ukraine, Trinidad & Tobago, Serbia & Montenegro, Ivory Coast and Ghana all rushed the gates. Of these, Ghana and the Ukraine both made it to the second round. Ghana lost 3-0 to Brazil in Dortmund, but the Ukraine won a penalty shoot-out after a 0-0 draw with Switzerland in Cologne. The Zhovto-Blakytni (Yellow-Blues) were then beaten 3-0 by Italy in Hamburg in the quarter-finals.

★ ★ ★

▦ FIVE NEARLY HOSTS

1 Argentina 1970 Mexico's facilities, built for the 1968 Olympics, gave them the edge over Argentina.

2 Colombia 1986 Chosen to host the 1986 tournament but were forced to resign due to a worsening financial situation.

3 USSR 1990 Came second to Italy.

4 South Africa 2006 After a controversial voting process, South Africa were edged out by Germany.

5 Morocco 2010 Finished four votes behind South Africa.

▦ VITAL PUB INFO

TO FOSTER FRIENDLY RELATIONS WITH FANS OF

ENGLAND

Fanspotter's guide

Check the mirror. Make sure you comb your hair and brush your teeth before pulling on the hallowed white nylon and representing your country, mind. Final touch: don't forget your lucky rosette, bobble hat or deely-boppers. There: bloody lovely.

Conversation starter

Not a lot of people know that shoelaces were invented in England in 1790. Or that shoes were invented shortly afterwards.

Accentuate the positive

With a win ratio of over 70 percent, coach Fabio Capello is comfortably England's greatest-ever manager in statistical terms, making previous leader Sir Alf Ramsey's 61 percent look positively sick by comparison.

Skirt expertly around the negative

No nation has ever won the World Cup with a foreign coach.

Form guide

Okay, so the second team lost to Brazil in a meaningless friendly; but it's important not to lose sight of how far Capello has brought England since December 2007. He's brought organisation and discipline to a team with options, who are now playing for each other. And he's brought England self-belief. Hasn't he?

One to watch

We've got a feeling: Jermain Defoe as the new Geoff Hurst.

Simply the best... ever

Bobby Moore – the only English skipper ever to lift the World Cup while team-mates jigged and cried and looked generally knackered. No excuses, no hard-luck stories, no penalties, no cheaty foreigners, no doubt.

Useful English phrases

'Ah, a penalty shoot-out. This is an exercise that relies heavily on an element of luck, and as such, both your team and your opponents have an equally strong chance of progressing to the next round.' – Ah, a penalty shoot-out. You'll be on the plane home in 20 minutes.

'Don't go all "Gazza" on me.' – Pull yourself together. Try to refrain from weeping uncontrollably (to be delivered after the inevitable anticlimax of a quarter-final exit).

'Who invited Emile Heskey?' – Who invited Emile Heskey?

Chat-up line

Shall I compare thee to a summer's day? Innit.

This one's on me

SOAP: What are you doing, Ed?

EDDY: Do you want one?

SOAP: No, I f*cking don't! You can't make a cup of tea, Edward.

EDDY: Why not? The whole of the British Empire was built on cups of tea.

SOAP: And look what happened to that.

EDDY: If you think I am going to war without one, you're mistaken, mate.

(*Lock, Stock & Two Smoking Barrels*, 1999)

Inside line on English culture

One of the more bizarre customs unique to England is that of 'cheese rolling'. This event usually takes place around the Spring Bank Holiday and involves several competitors chasing a round cheese down a steep hill. The first person to grab the speeding ball of fermented milk is the winner. The 'sport' is as hazardous as it is baffling, and many entrants end up with their arms, legs – and general sense of self-worth – badly damaged.

Common ground

George Orwell suggested: 'The English are not happy unless they are miserable.' That's the great thing about World Cups: they're win-win.

★ ★ ★

▦ TALKING A GOOD GAME

Willie Ormond,
Scotland manager,
1974

All we have to do to qualify for the second stage is beat Brazil.

⠿ WORLD CUP SONGS
SPAIN 1982

England World Cup Squad – 'This Time (We'll Get It Right)'
(Number 2)
The choice sample here is the stripped-down folkie opening bars, with accordion and circus drum leading into the squad's clenched-fist mission statement: 'We're on our way / We are Ron's twenty-two...' Thereafter, the kitchen sink production piles up oompah, a vast orchestral nod to *Dambusters*, crowd chants and even a calypso syn-drum breakdown as the blokes seem to get steadily shriller as the Germans loom. 'Hear the roar / Of the red, white and blue...'

Shame they didn't have the balls to let chorus-leader Kevin Keegan loose on a follow-up to his classy Anglo-disco hit 'Head Over Heels In Love'. The FA's resolute failure to acknowledge disco, punk or even New Romanticism was partly tempered on the *This Time We'll Get It Right* LP, where Justin Fashanu's frankly astonishing 'Do It 'Cos You Like It' predated the thrust of Frankie Goes To Hollywood's 'Relax' by at least a year.

Meanwhile, the 1982 Scotland World Cup Squad made number 5 in the charts with 'We Have a Dream'. More accurately, they swayed a bit in the background while John Gordon Sinclair recalled a dream about them winning. It was a poor old attempt to cash in on *Gregory's Girl*. Dare we suggest Clare Grogan and Altered Images might have made a more rousing anthem to nocturnal teenage reveries and ultimate disappointment?

Cliff Portwood and the 1966 World Cup Squad – 'Up There England'
(Failed to chart)
Recorded in 1982, ex-footballer Portwood's song is a true England classic, but one which has since become shrouded in controversy. That's because it was included on the Cherry Red Records compilation CD *England's Glory – England Squads and Supporters*, which claimed 'The legendary England football song started in 1970, with Cliff Portwood encouraging members of the '66 squad to join him for "Up There England" and "You'll Never Walk Alone"...' In that case, this little-known cheesy gem would have helped define the football song formula, with the cabaret crooner's tear-jerking observations on the nobility of the game giving way to booming oompah mode, and a slightly flat, manful chorus doing battle with taped crowd noises. But this was no groundbreaker. In fact, it was based (without credit) on the huge Australian hit of 1979, 'Up There Cazaly' by Two-Man Band, penned by Mike Brady.

In 1997, the song was again reworked as 'Steve Bloomer's Watchin' by Derby County fans Mark Tewson and Martyn Miller, and recorded by actor Robert 'Wolfie Smith' Lindsay. Ever since, the anthem has been played at Pride Park when the Rams take to the field.

Once Tom Finney's deputy at Preston North End, Cliff Portwood played for Port Vale, Grimsby and Portsmouth between 1959 and 1969, then emigrated to South Africa, turning out for Durban United before embarking on a singing career that saw him make five gold albums, becoming a star in Australia and the USA. He got permission to record the song in 1982 via his mate in Mike Brady's backing band, but it went unreleased because of copyright issues surrounding the B-side, which included chunks of 'Land of Hope and Glory'. It has long been a mystery to football fans and record collectors alike.

★ ★ ★

▦ WHAT THE PAPERS SAY
1970 WORLD CUP

Forty years after the first World Cup, things had moved on. The official World Cup brochure in Mexico was a more sophisticated affair, but still had a way to go, compared with what we see now, 40 years later:

Cover A photo of a blue, beige and white Earth projects a 3D '1970' with as much dynamism as a 1970s graphic can. Produced by Hunter Collier – 8 Shillings or 40p.

Introduction by Sir Stanley Rous CBE: 'Although the World Cup is comparatively youthful against the full background of football history, it has become established as the Premier Award in international football honours in four decades.'

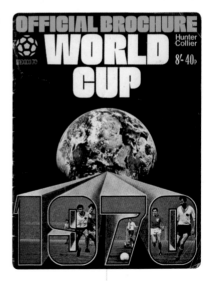

Not a magazine but a bro...sssssshhhhhure.

History • A brief rundown of the previous eight tournaments:

■ **1930** – These teams faced an adventurous sea voyage to Montevideo – passenger aircraft capable of making an Atlantic crossing were still very much in the future...

■ **1934** – The confident Italians, fielding a team of doubtful 'nationals' – at least half the side were Argentinians – relied on robust physical power...

■ **1938** – Hitler had occupied Austria, and Spain was locked in civil war. It was an uneasy and strangely discordant tournament...

■ **1950** – The United States had nothing to lose and so it began: England failed, time after time, to finish what they had started; crippling anxiety set in and the Americans snatched an astonishing victory...

■ **1954** – Puskas, his fitness still in doubt, returned for the final; at his best he might have saved Hungary but the unseeded West Germany held their 3-2 lead. The World Cup was back in Europe...

■ **1958** – Astonishing. Unbelievable. Dazzling. Pelé was all of these things. Sweden had no answer to his infinite virtuosity...

■ **1962** – Catenaccio was dedicated to absolute security, its sole basis being to destroy the opposition. Catenaccio hung sullenly over the 1962 tournament in Chile, producing tedious, negative, often ruthless football.

■ **1966** – Alan Ball threw every last ounce of stamina into a blistering run down the right wing; he crossed to Hurst who hit the ball against the underside of the crossbar. The Germans exploded in protest – had the ball come down over the goal-line?

Guide to Mexico – Short pictorial travelogue of Mexico... Aztec heritage... clean new architecture... donkeys... markets... and a swift tour of the five stadia, including the magnificent, 105,000 capacity Azteca in Mexico City.

Guide to the Teams – Someone from each team is asked about its prospects:

■ **Belgium** – Raymond Goethals, trainer: 'I don't expect us to reach the quarter-finals. Our country is too small to do more than that.'

■ **Sweden** – Orvar Bergmark, manager: 'I believe we will raise a few eyebrows.'

Israel – Emmanuel Sheffer, national coach: 'The football is round and anything can happen.'

England – Sir Alf Ramsey, manager: 'I believe it will take a very good team indeed to take the World Cup away from England.'

Brazil – Joao Saldanha, coach: 'We have been in tougher groups before. If England's prospects are excellent then so are ours.'

Czechoslovakia – Josef Marko, manager: 'We shall play zonal defence

against England... but attack the Brazilians immediately they get the ball.'
Morocco – Blagoje Vidinic, trainer: 'When they get into a stadium with 100,000 spectators they might get wobbly knees.'
Advert 'Collect a set of 30 World Cup coins from your Esso Action Station.'

★ ★ ★

▦ TOTALLY UNBIASED FIFA WORLD CUP RULES

■ **Article 16.3** In the case of any discrepancy in the interpretation of the Laws of the Game, the English version is authoritative.

★ ★ ★

▦ VITAL PUB INFO
TO FOSTER FRIENDLY RELATIONS WITH FANS OF

USA

Fanspotter's guide
Big, loveable, friendly, happy puppies with beer helmets (m) and spangly pointy bras (f – to be specific, Madonna and Wonder Woman).
Conversation starter
Did you know Wolves won the first-ever North American Soccer League in the summer of 1967, playing as the LA Wolves?
Accentuate the positive
Ranked 14 by FIFA (and still basking in an all-time high of being ranked at No 4 in 2006) and ever-present at the World Cup since the 1990 finals...
Skirt expertly around the negative
... Chiefly because (aside from fellow qualifiers Mexico and Honduras), the biggest threat in the CONCACAF qualifying division comes from the Canadian 'Puck-kicker' Soccerdudes, the combined might of Trinidad & Tobago, and the Jamaican bobsleigh team.
Form guide
In June 2009, Tim Howard, Clint Dempsey & Co beat Spain 2-0 in the

Confederations Cup in South Africa, ending their record 35-game unbeaten run. And they only lost 3-2 to Brazil in the final.

One to watch

Oguchi Onyewu – the towering Inter Milan centre-back recently signed from Standard Liege (via 11 games on loan at Newcastle).

Simply the best... ever

A handful of games in four years at Bayer Leverkusen, and the same on loan at Bayern Munich. Translated into American, that means Landon Donovan can claim a place on the Major League Soccer's all-time scoring list, and multiple US Soccer Athlete of the Year awards. Recently formed an offensive partnership with Becks at LA Galaxy, he joined Everton on loan in January.

Useful American phrases

'Y'all are down one-zero at the end of the third quarter' – You're losing 1-0 in the 70th minute.

'Hell of a headshot from the MVP! It's in the back of the goal-bag!' – A star player has scored with a header.

Chat-up line

The average American female weighs 163 pounds. As such, the average American male is probably looking elsewhere.

This one's on me

Three and a half gallons of full-fat Coca-Cola.

Inside line on American culture

'Soccer drains America of the next generation's talent in the sports that really matter. No other activity in life requires so much effort for so little reward. The least offensive-minded game ever invented, [soccer represents] the Marxist concept of the labor theory of value applied to sports – which may explain why socialist nations dominate in the World Cup.' – Stephen Moore, 'Soccer-mom Hell', *National Review*, May 1998.

Common ground

American President Barack Obama is a West Ham fan. Though how he often he actually gets to games, we're not sure.

★ ★ ★

ENGLAND STARS AND THEIR WAGS

- David Beckham and Victoria Beckham
- Wayne Rooney and Coleen Rooney
- Peter Crouch and Abigail Clancy
- Ashley Cole and Cheryl Cole
- Theo Walcott and Melanie Slade
- Steven Gerrard and Alex Curran
- Bobby Moore and Tina Moore
- Billy Wright and Joy Beverley (of the Beverley Sisters)

England's 2006 World Cup tie against Trinidad & Tobago attracted a glittering line-up of authors: Coleen McLoughlin is seated behind Cheryl Tweedy and Victoria Beckham.

★ ★ ★

TALKING A GOOD GAME

Austrian striker Josef Bican on their defeat to Italy in 1934, quoted in *World Cup Stories*, Chris Hunt (2006)

> They were little crooks, they used to cheat a little, no they used to cheat a lot... The referee even played for them. When I passed the ball out to the right wing one of our players, Cicek, ran for it and the referee headed it back to the Italians. It was unbelievable.

WHATEVER HAPPENED TO THE HEROES?

George Cohen • England 1966

George Best described Cohen as 'the best full-back I ever played against', while England boss Alf Ramsey dubbed him 'England's greatest right-back'. Not bad for a player who served Fulham loyally from 1956-69, notching up 459 appearances and 37 caps before injury ended his career. He later coached Fulham youth and England Under-23s, and beat a 14-year bout of stomach cancer in the 1980s. Rewarded with a tardy recognition of his Cup-lifting exploits with the MBE in 2000, George now acts as host at the George Cohen Restaurant at Fulham's Craven Cottage. A winner.

George wasn't the best Al-Fayed body double but he still got a small badge for it.

Joe Gaetjens • USA 1950

When a strong England side lost to a team of part-timers from the USA in 1950, it provided perhaps the biggest shock in World Cup history. Haitian Joe Gaetjens scored the only goal of the game, but broke FIFA rules. In those days, the intention to become a US citizen was enough to qualify you for playing for that nation, but Joe never did become an American. Retrospectively, the match was undeniably England's – a controversy which palls into insignificance given Joe's tragic fate. Fourteen years after his moment of fame, Gaetjens was arrested by the Haitian secret police, the Tontons Macoutes, and went missing in jail, presumed murdered.

Wlodzimierz Lubanski • Poland 1978
Lubanski was nominated by the PZPN (Polish FA) as their most outstanding player of the past 50 years, scoring 50 goals in 80 internationals. In England, we remember only the disastrous Wembley (non-)qualifier against Poland; but in their earlier 2-0 win in Chorzow, Lubanski robbed Bobby Moore to score before being badly injured by a Roy McFarland hack, which cost him the two best

years of his career. It was great to see him return for the 1978 finals; but Poland couldn't repeat their third-place finish. Wlodek played most of his club career at Górnik Zabrze, winning seven Polish championships. He finished his career at Belgian club Lokeren, where he still coaches the strikers.

The Polish legend was also nominated in the most difficult name to spell category but just lost out to Borussia Dortmund midfielder Jakub Blaszczykowski.

★ ★ ★

▦ TALKSPORT'S ALL-TIME BEST ENGLAND WORLD CUP XI

This is the team that was voted for by the readers of talkSPORT.net/mag.

1 Gordon Banks England's World Cup-winning keeper and iconic Pelé-foiler. But did you know 'Banks of England' was transfer-listed by Leicester City just a year after his 1966 heroics, due to the emergence of 17-year-old prodigy Peter Shilton?

2 Des Walker England's greatest centre-half in recent history suffered only one poor season in his career, at Sampdoria in 1992-93. The name of the manager stupid enough to play him at left-back? Sven.

3 Stuart Pearce Twelve years to amass 78 England caps; 12 years to notch up 522 inspirational appearances for Nottingham Forest. But how many fans remember 'Psycho' also played more than 30 League games each for Coventry City, Newcastle United, West Ham and Man City?

4 Bobby Moore The image of young Bobby holding the World Cup aloft is English football's most iconic moment. That said; you must search YouTube for Mooro's ace TV ad trumpeting the glories of the pub ('Look in at your Local!').

5 John Terry Most fans think of Terry as a 'one-club man' for Chelsea, or possibly even as 'Captain Controversy'; but did you know he also made six League appearances on loan at Nottingham Forest in 2000?

6 Paul Gascoigne Ten goals in ten years in an England shirt, nine weeks on the chart with Lindisfarne and 'Fog On The Tyne' in 1990 ... and 39 days as Kettering Town boss in 2005.

7 David Beckham England's most-capped outfield player (115 appearances, 17 goals) made his League debut not for Manchester United, but during a loan spell at Preston (5 appearances, 2 goals).

Bobby Moore, England's inspirational World Cup-winning captain, leads out his team to take on Argentina.

8 Sir Stanley Matthews Not a lot of people know that Stoke and Blackpool's 'Wizard of the Dribble' enjoyed the longest career of any England player, stretching from 1934 to 1957.

9 Sir Bobby Charlton England's all-time record scorer with 49 goals, beating Gary Lineker into second place with 48. But did you know it took Charlton 26 more games than Lineker to get that one extra goal?

10 Sir Geoff Hurst Best remember Sir Geoff for his cracking average of 24 goals in his 49 England internationals rather than for his short-lived re-emergence as Chelsea boss in 1979.

11 Gary Lineker According to talkSPORT stats, in his 16 goalbanging years at Leicester, Everton, Barcelona, Spurs and Nagoya, Gary was hacked down 679,000 times – never once retaliating to earn a yellow card.

▦ VITAL PUB INFO
TO FOSTER FRIENDLY RELATIONS WITH FANS OF

ALGERIA

Fanspotter's guide

Algeria is 90 percent Sahara desert. Look out for thirsty fans in white shirts with green trim.

Conversation starter

In the 1800s, Algeria was a renowned base for pirates and slave traders. France invaded the country in 1827, after a French consul was struck in the face with a whisk by the ruler of Algiers. But surely that was no grounds to invade the country? Just get him in the chin with a potato peeler and call it quits.

Accentuate the positive

Rabah Saadane is currently enjoying his fifth stint as national coach.

Skirt expertly around the negative

Saadane was coach in 1986 when Algeria bombed out, but sadly not in their debut finals of 1982 when they should have progressed beyond the group stage – and would have, had Germany and Austria not conspired to play out a draw to ensure they both went through.

Form guide

Successfully overcame minnows Zambia and Rwanda in African qualifying Group C, but needed a play-off to get the better of Egypt – this despite three players getting injured when their bus was stoned on the way to the stadium, before a victory that sparked violence across North Africa, resulting in a dozen deaths. Egypt got their revenge in the African Cup of Nations, beating Algeria 4-0 in the semi-final.

Two to watch

VfL Bochum centre-half Antar Yahia is not only solid at the back – his rocket volley from a narrow angle against Egypt put Algeria in the finals and made him top scorer in the qualifiers. Karim Ziani also plays in Germany, as playmaker for Wolfsburg.

Simply the best... ever

If only Algerians played for Algeria instead of France, they could claim Zidane. Meanwhile, superlative-prone Man City boss Kevin Keegan called Ali Benarbia 'the best player I've ever worked with'. The true great is celebrated FC Porto striker Rabah Madjer, Algeria's all-time top scorer (with 31 in 87 appearances), and present at both their previous finals appearances. He's also been national coach, though only three times!

Useful Algerian phrases

فـقـوم حرشل يـنـلأسـت لا طـقف .كتـغـل يف ةيـساسألا تالماجملا لدابت عيـطتسأ
تسلل ةدعاقلا – I can exchange basic pleasantries in your language. Just don't
ask me to explain the offside rule.

أنت تحدي ايـل؟ – Are you challenging me?

ءاوس دح ىلع هيـضراعم ىلا بـرقا ناك اذإ للـست فـقوم يف بـعالا لاقو .ادج ديج
نم طخ املرمى ىلكتا ةركلاو مصخلاو يناثلا املاضي. كيـف فـيك تريد هل مـه لتـفاحا؟ – Very
well. A player is in an offside position if he is nearer to his opponents' goal
line than both the ball and the second last opponent. How do you like
them apples?

Chat-up line

Algeria is one of the top three cork-producing countries in the world,
alongside Spain and Portugal. And you are a corker.

This one's on me

Mint teas all round.

Inside line on Algerian culture

Algeria is home to the biggest sand dunes in the world. They can be found in
the Sahara desert and are up to 430m (1,411ft) high. That's nearly twice the
height of Canary Wharf, we'll have you know.

Common ground

In the south of France, Paris and – if you know where to head – London, the
Algerian tagine is an alternative to the Asian curry. A rich, thick meat and
vegetable stew, as hot and spicy as you like it.

★ ★ ★

▦ TEN MISSED PENALTIES

1 The last kick of the 1994 World Cup tournament saw Roberto Baggio
send his penalty kick sailing over the bar, which meant that Brazil had won
the trophy for the first time in 24 years. It was the first occasion that the
tournament had been decided by a penalty shoot-out. 'My plan was to lift
the ball..., but not to that extent,' Baggio explained.

2 The 1990 semi-final between England and West Germany stood at 1-1 after
extra time. Gary Lineker, Peter Beardsley and David Platt all found the net, but
Stuart Pearce's effort, straight down the middle, was saved by Bodo Illgner as
Pearce became the first England player to fail to score in a penalty shoot-out...

3 ... Olaf Thon beat Peter Shilton to put Germany 4-3 up, so when Chris Waddle missed the target England's second most successful World Cup campaign was over.

The thing that still hurts is that Illgner was doing his best to dive out of the way.

4 England again exited the tournament after a penalty shoot-out in France 1998. A thrilling 2-2 draw against Argentina had to be settled from the penalty spot. It was advantage England when David Seaman tipped Hernan Crespo's spot kick round the right-hand post, but then Paul Ince had his penalty saved by Carlos Roa.

5 ... Paul Merson and Michael Owen then scored, but so did the Argentinians, meaning it was 4-3 when David Batty stepped up to take the last penalty. He placed his kick too close to Roa and England were out.

6 After 120 minutes of a goalless quarter-final of the 2006 World Cup against Portugal in Gelsenkirchen came that moment England fans had to come to loathe and fear... the penalty shoot-out – and this was their worst attempt to date. Frank Lampard took the first penalty, and had his effort saved by Ricardo...

7 ... Owen Hargreaves then scored to level up things, before Steven Gerrard was denied by a carbon copy save by Ricardo, low to his left. After three penalties each, it was 1-1...

8 ... Postiga scored next, before Jamie Carragher planted the ball into the net. But the referee cruelly indicated that he had not blown his whistle and made him take it again. His second attempt was scooped up by the grounded keeper and bounced up onto the bar. Cristiano Ronaldo beat Paul Robinson and it was *auf wiedersehen* England once again.

9 Here's one that didn't matter. The 1986 quarter-final in Guadalajara between France and Brazil ended all square at 1-1. The only Frenchman to miss his penalty was Michel Platini who launched his spot kick over the bar, over the fence and into the jubilant Brazil fans behind the goal. However, both Socrates and Julio Cesar missed, so France went through. No harm done, except maybe a dent in the maestro's pride.

10 As the 1994 World Cup opening ceremony approached its climax, Diana Ross, dressed in a violently scarlet outfit, marched down the middle of the pitch towards a ball placed on the penalty spot. She swung wildly at it with her right peg and sent it scuttling along the ground, well wide of the left-hand post. The crossbar then split in half and the goal fell in two, presumably with the force of her shot, as it was intended in the script. It was a farce. This was the World Cup that was bookended by two missed penalties – see No 1.

★ ★ ★

▦ FIVE WORLD CUP DOGS

1 Pickles – who famously sniffed out the Jules Rimet trophy from its hiding place in a South London hedge after it had been stolen in the run-up to the 1966 tournament.

2 Bi – who invaded the pitch during the 1962 quarter-final between Brazil and England in Chile. Jimmy Greaves managed to catch him, where others had failed, but was rewarded with a stream of canine urine down his shirt. Brazilian star Garrincha thought this was very amusing and adopted the incontinent stray.

3 Unknown – After losing to Peru and drawing with Iran in 1978, Scotland manager Ally McLeod was sitting with journalists in the grounds of the squad's hotel. When approached by a stray mongrel, McLeod sombrely observed: 'This little fellow is my last friend in the world', before bending down to pat him. The dog immediately bit his hand.

4 Winston – A live bulldog who accompanied the England side to Mexico 1970 as their lucky mascot.

Bobby Charlton and Colin Bell take time out to make unkind comments about a sad-looking animal. Norman Hunter allegedly furious.

5 Bulldog Bobby – By the time England next qualified for the World Cup, in 1982, a real bulldog had been replaced by a cartoon one wearing a broad grin and an Admiral England strip. Some journalists doubted the wisdom of using a dog associated with aggression while England fans were busy tearing up half of Europe, but he seemed quite popular. He bore more than a passing resemblance to Spike, Tom the cat's nemesis in the *Tom & Jerry* cartoons.

★ ★ ★

ENGLAND'S MOST CRUCIAL WORLD CUP QUALIFIERS

Republic of Ireland 1   England 1 • 19 May 1957

No matter that they'd beaten Ireland 5-1 the week before, our boys still needed a 90th-minute equaliser to avoid a bottom-clenching play-off.

England 2   Portugal 0 • 25 October 1961

It was scary news when 'hopeless' Luxembourg beat 'superb' Portugal, meaning we needed a point to qualify. [See page 22 for match report]

England 1   Poland 1 • 17 October 1973

England had lost 2-0 away, and Bobby Moore looked past it, humiliated by the quicksilver Lubanski. But the media still had blind faith and reckoned we'd walk it. Cloughie's 'clown' comments about Poland keeper Jan Tomaszewski still haunt us, as does Shilton's failure to stick his foot out to stop Domarski's shot in Poland's only attack of the game. Then there was the last-minute header off the line from sub Kevin Hector's attempt. And so no World Cup for 12 years between 1970 and 1982.

England 1   Hungary 0 • 18 November 1981

Just a point was required, which England duly chalked up; though hardly in convincing fashion, as Paul Mariner turned in Trevor Brooking's mishit shot.

Poland 0   England 0 • 11 October 1989

Redemption time for Peter Shilton. Sixteen years after failing to beat Poland at Wembley, this time we made it, scraping the vital point we needed to qualify! Best draw a veil over Poland hitting the bar in the last minute, for the sake of any dodgy tickers out there...

Italy 0   England 0 • 11 October 1997

England's best performance under Glenn Hoddle. Hardly a goal fest, but how sweet to remember Gianfranco Zola having to eat his words: 'Italy never make mistakes on the big occasion.' During the match, Ian Wright missed a penalty, which would have eased the situation. However, Hoddle's controversial faith-healer Eileen Drewery apparently claimed that she had willed him to miss, fearing that an England goal could have sparked a riot.

England 2   Greece 2 • 6 October 2001

England needed a win to ensure qualification, so it made us just a tad twitchy to twice fall behind. Beckham's last-minute free-kick salvaged a barely deserved point at Old Trafford. And, phew! Germany had been held at home by Finland!

Lucky this game was played at Old Trafford, where last-minute (and indeed 97th-minute) goals are not unknown.

★ ★ ★

▦ VITAL PUB INFO
TO FOSTER FRIENDLY RELATIONS WITH FANS OF

SLOVENIA

Fanspotter's guide
Listen out for groups clad in Nike white, apparently discussing Bill and Ben the Flowerpot Men (the Slovenian capital is called Ljubljana).

Conversation starter
Small world. The Slovenian skipper Robert Koren plays in midfield for West Brom.

Accentuate the positive
Came ahead of pre-qualifying favourites Poland and Czech Republic in the qualifiers, even though they did come second to Slovakia.

Skirt expertly around the negative
A team of famously elegant, high-trotting, white Lipizzaner showhorses

(originating from Lipica in Slovenia) would be no less likely to lift the World Cup.

Form guide

Ooyer, look out! Maybe England's 'easy group' opener won't be so much of a cakewalk. The Slovenians beat Russia in the play-offs on the strength of a precious away goal in Moscow, which they followed up with a 1-0 win in Maribor. This team has balls.

One to watch

Milivoje 'Supernova' Novakovic – inspirational striker with 13 goals in 36 international appearances, was sacked as captain of Cologne for sticking around to enjoy the vast government-funded party that followed victory over the Russians. Good lad, Milivoje!

Simply the best... ever

Zlatko Zahovic – attacking midfielder who won national league titles with FK Partizan (Serbia), Porto and Benfica (Portugal) and Olympiakos (Greece), and a Champions League runner-up medal with Valencia in 2001.

Useful Slovene phrases

Vstopi! – Come in!

Sezuj se! – Take your shoes off!

Dosti! – That's enough!

Obleci se! – Get dressed!

Chat-up line

Zajtrk za dva, prosim – I would like to have breakfast for two, please.

This one's on me

Situated between Italy and Hungary, there's more to Slovenian wine than the Riesling they export. Large reds all round!

Inside line on Slovenian culture

FYR Slovenia has the lowest marriage rate in all the EU. '*Pojdem Na Štajersko*' is a popular Slovenian folk (aka drinking) song that centres on a young bloke's trip to Styria to see his three girlfriends, each in turn specialising in drink, food and how's-your-father. All together now!

Pojdem na Štajersko

Gledat, kaj delajo,

Gledat, kaj delajo

Ljubice tri...

Common ground

The snow-capped Alps, the deep azure Adriatic, the hilltops dotted with white chapels and historic castles... squint a bit, and Slovenia is pretty much like Wales.

▓ PICK OF THE WORLD CUP POPS

The inside line on tracks from the 1970 England World Cup Squad's LP, *The World Beaters Sing The World Beaters* – taken direct from the sleevenotes inside the curious circular gatefold package.

Side One

'Back Home'

A sincere performance from the players on what looks like becoming a 'standard' song.

'Sugar Sugar'

Bobby Moore leading the players in a sensational version of this million seller. Listen for Francis Lee in the last verse.

'Lovey-Dovey'

Your actual 'reggae' music with Gordon Banks in true Caribbean form.

1970 Album cash-in. *The World Beaters Sing the World Beaters*. Do you see what they've done there? The sleeve is quite natty, though – a triple, gatefold, football-shaped thing Who could ask for more?

'Lily The Pink'

Chorus is sung with tremendous sensitivity, solos on the verses being taken by Geoff Hurst, Jeff Astle and Peter Bonetti.

'You're In My Arms'

Jeff Astle leads the lads in a good old sentimental singalong.

'Puppet On A String'

The first British song ever to win the Eurovision Song Contest is served up with a Mexican flavour by the first British team ever to win the World Cup.

Side Two

'Congratulations'

Let's hope this is the song everyone will be singing after Mexico.

'Ob-La-Di Ob-La-Da'

This was definitely the captain's showcase, Bobby does a fine solo run assisted by Norman Hunter, Terry Cooper, Tommy Wright and Martin Peters.

'Glory-O'
A song with a message from all the boys.
'Make Me An Island'
Everton and Liverpool get together at last. Alan Ball and Emlyn Hughes combine to form a great singing duo.
'Cinnamon Stick'
Brian Labone and Francis Lee let their hair down on this 'bubblegum' song.
'There'll Always Be An England'
A stirring performance by the entire squad with a special word from Bobby Moore, Alan Ball and Bobby Charlton.
© Pye Records 1970

★ ★ ★

▦ TALKING A GOOD GAME

Vittorio Pozzo, Italian coach in 1938

Our players don't even dream to make some politics, but the fascist salute is the official flag of the moment, it's a sort of ceremony and they must show allegiance to it. I have my ideas, but I know what my duty is. When we take to the field we are solemn and deafening hisses attend us. And we don't lower the hand until the hisses are stopped. The action of intimidation has not succeeded.

⠿ SUPERFANS

Ken Bailey, England

Ken eventually overcame his natural reluctance to make an exhibition of himself.

Ken was a self-appointed, unofficial mascot who wore a John Bull outfit of Union Jack waistcoat and top hat. He also carried the torch at the 1948 London Olympics, and was a local Conservative councillor in Bournemouth. Ken had the supreme honour of having a Subbuteo figure made in his image. He also had his topper knocked off by angry Argentinians in Spain 82, upset about the Falklands. He waded in among them trying to spread his message of international peace, love and sportsmanship, but they took him all wrong. The rotters.

The Bird Man, Colombia

Gustav Llanos, a law graduate and priest from Colombia, dresses in a startling, sequinned yellow, red and blue condor costume. He was inspired by a dream in 1986 that he had been divinely chosen to become Colombia's official mascot and to help his team to World Cup glory, and set out to fulfil what he felt was a spiritual mission. He nearly came to a sticky end in Italy in 1990 when Freddy Rincon equalised for Colombia in the last minute against West Germany in Milan. Gustav liked to be strapped into a special harness and hung from the front of an upper tier stand so that he could flap about in the manner of a condor. With his mates celebrating the goal, they all let go of him at the same time and he ended up in the tier below. Fortunately he (and the people below him) emerged unscathed and Gustav viewed his lucky escape as divine intervention. Well, he would.

The Tartan Army, Scotland

'We are not an organisation, rather, we are a disorganisation...' Followers of Scotland were among worst-behaved supporters in the world in the 1970s, notorious for leaving Trafalgar Square knee deep in beer cans; tearing up the Wembley turf; and taking the goalposts 'hame'. They upset their German hosts with some boisterous beer-hall behaviour in 1974 with a Frankfurt bandleader announcing: 'You are not in Scotland now. This is orderly Germany! Behave gentlemen.'

The Bay City Rollers were never charged, but their sartorial legacy can still be seen in Scotland today.

The Scots gradually adopted a code of exemplary behaviour, while England's followers moved in the opposite direction in the 80s. They are now seen as ambassadors for the Scottish game, but sadly their appearances in the finals have now dried up.

Manolo el del Bombo, Spain

Valencia fan Manolo is utterly devoted to the Spanish national side. He is known worldwide for his large, deafening drum and his rousing: 'Boom boom boom, ES-PAN-YA!' Manolo hitch-hiked 15,800km around Spain following his team in the 1982 tournament and has not missed a World Cup since then. But he has paid a big price for his loyalty. He returned home from a match in 1987 to discover that his entire family had left him. Boom boom.

The Red Devils, South Korea

In the mid-1990s some previously staid supporters of South Korea made a conscious decision to give their team a more vocal and passionate backing. They adopted the nickname 'Red Devils', wore devil horns, T-shirts with the slogan 'Be the Reds!' and kicked up a racket with their buks (Korean drums) and thundersticks. By the time they co-hosted the tournament in 2002, this had taken off in a big way and their games were played against an almost exclusively red and noisy backdrop. The Red Devils tend to be younger than your average set of fans, and with more females, which is audibly confirmed when South Korea score to be greeted with a noise only previously heard at Beatles concerts.

The Oranje, Netherlands

Followers of the Netherlands have long been known for turning up in synchronised clothing for games, usually forming startling banks of orange within stadia all over the globe. This came unstuck in Germany 2006 when the Oranje were literally caught with their trousers down. Many Dutch supporters turned up to their game against the Ivory Coast in Stuttgart wearing bright orange lederhosen, available as a promotional item from Dutch beer makers Bavaria (proof of purchase of just 12 cans and they are yours for €7.95). They had a lion's tail protruding out of the back and were a smash hit in fashion-challenged Holland. But FIFA judged them to be 'ambush marketing', an attempt to get free advertising by anyone other than an official sponsor, and over 1,000 fans were debagged before going into the ground. One disgruntled fan told the media: 'I watched the game in my pants – fortunately I had quite a long T-shirt.'

The Full-on Brazilians

Pity the poor TV cameraman on his month-long World Cup jolly, plucked from the heart of his loving family and forced to jog down the touchline

carrying one of those funny grass-eye-view cameras on a pole – or worse still, put on the dreaded 'local colour' detail, scanning the stands with his telephoto lens for suicidal expressions and amusing headgear. When Brazil are playing, the cameraman's job is made easiest of all because the prime targets are all wearing bright yellow crop T-shirts emblazoned (sometimes deceptively) with the letters 'BRA'. It's like shooting fish in a barrel. It's almost as if every female beach volleyball club in the nation had been ordered to come along in their uniform hot-pants/bikini bottoms/thongs. They samba. They jiggle. They squeal in unexpected excitement at the beginning of the first half, having forgotten about the change of ends. And that's just the cameramen.

Brazilian fans: marginally more popular than Leeds and Millwall supporters.

★ ★ ★

▦ TALKING A GOOD GAME

> **We're naturally delighted to be in the semi-final. It's unbelievable – well, it's not unbelievable, we believe it all right.**

Bobby Robson, quoted in *All Played Out,* Pete Davies (1990)

▥ VITAL PUB INFO
TO FOSTER FRIENDLY RELATIONS WITH FANS OF

GERMANY

Fanspotter's guide

Look out for the towels efficiently laid out in Hyde Park on the morning of Germany's big kick-off against Australia.

Conversation starter

You're right. It wasn't quite over the line, was it?

Accentuate the positive

After winning the World Cup in 1990, Germany twice reached the quarter-finals, then finished runners-up to Brazil in Japan/Korea, and then came third last time around on home soil. Second again in the 2008 Euros, which lends them a sense of momentum.

Skirt expertly around the negative

Ranked No 6 by FIFA, Germany look odds-on to fare extremely well again. And ultimately fail.

Form guide

Qualified with relative ease ahead of Russia, Finland and Wales, beating the Russkies 1-0 in Moscow to make it official.

One to watch

Cologne striker Lukas Podolski, still aged just 24, already has goal stats (37 in 69 appearances) to compare with those of his strike partner Miroslav Klose (48 in 93), his senior by seven years.

Simply the best… ever

Franz Beckenbauer was both a World Cup winner and runner-up in his distinguished career as a libero defender and national coach. Lothar Matthäus has played more World Cup games than anyone else, 25 strung between 1982 and 1998. Gerd Mueller was the all-time record World Cup scorer before he was overtaken by Ronaldo.

Useful German phrases

Unsere Völker haben ihre Probleme in der Vergangenheit hatten. Wenden wir uns nun stellen diese hinter uns und genießen Sie diese wunderbare Sportspektakel wie reife Erwachsene – Our nations have had their problems in the past. Let us now put these behind us and enjoy this wonderful sporting spectacle like mature adults.

Zwei Weltkriege und eine Weltmeistershaft. Doo Dah. Doo Dah – Two World Wars and one World Cup. Doo Dah. Doo Dah.

Chat-up line

According to German tradition, it is good luck to meet a chimney sweep in the street. But surely it's even better luck to meet a man in private with an extendable handle on his brush?

This one's on me

A stein of Weissbier and a snifter of Schnapps.

Inside line on German culture

BALDRICK: I've heard what these Germans will do, sir. They'll have their wicked way with anything of woman born.

BLACKADDER: Well, in that case, Baldrick, you're quite safe. However, the Teutonic reputation for brutality is well-founded: their operas last three or four days. They have no word for 'fluffy'.

(*Blackadder Goes Forth*, 1989)

Common ground

The Brits and Germans both have a reflex distaste for children with stupid names – 'Peaches' or 'Pixie', right Bob? – but only one of the nations has decided to give legal protection to their potential 'Dweezils' and 'Moon Units'. By German law, a child's name must: a) reflect the sex of the child (taxi for John 'Marion' Wayne?) and b) not endanger the 'well-being of the child'. A German couple who were hoping to honour their favourite American actress by naming their luckless newborn 'Whoopi' had their application rejected because, among other things, the name resembles the English expression 'to make whoopee'.

★ ★ ★

▦ WORLD CUP SONGS
MEXICO 1986

England World Cup Squad – 'We Got The Whole World At Our Feet'
(Number 66)

Oh lordy, surely by 1986 we could do better than yet more shuffling footballers on *Top of the Pops*, all booted and suited and clenching their arses under Captain Marvel's homicidally patriotic lead? Ripping off an earlier Notts Forest & Paper Lace single atrocity – 'There's Spider and Needham, they'll never yield / There's Archie the Gemmill all over the field' – this effort made Cloughie's mob seem like a bunch of soulful street poets. The end of an era.

By comparison Colourbox's 'Official World Cup Theme' pointed the way forward, a brave commission featuring a tune and some actual relevance. The bleeding-edge Young brothers whipped up a juddering BBC Radiophonic Workshop *Doctor Who* vibe, heavy on primitive synths and new-fangled hip-hop samples. Bear in mind, this was a year before their revolutionary 'Pump Up The Volume', and two years before the Timelords scored a hit with the eerily similar 'Doctorin' The Tardis'.

Yet more bleeding edge was the Scotland World Cup Squad, whose 'Big Trip To Mexico' was a huge mariachi-driven street party of a record, as envisioned by a sound engineer who had never set foot south or west of Lossiemouth: 'We're the squad, you know us all by name / We'll give all we've got to bring the trophy hame...' And you never knew World Music was invented north of the border?

★ ★ ★

▦ WHAT THE PAPERS SAY
1982 WORLD CUP

In Spain, *Match Weekly* had its own take on the events it had seen during that summer's tournament. Its 17 July edition cost 35p and inside were the following stories:

The bonuses for success had not yet quite made it to today's level as Paolo Rossi, the Prodigal Son of Italian football, found out. Delighted with Italy's win, an Italian shoemaker has given Rossi and his family enough shoes to last a lifetime; while another fan made a gift of 1,000 bottles of wine.

'Time to Move On' is the title of the Kevin Keegan column. Kev reckons: 'Once again, I have a yearning to play my football in

a foreign country... I'm not going to go out looking for clubs, I'll let the world come to me.' Bobby Robson would take him at his word, bringing Keegan's international career to a swift end.

Steve Coppell is still a bit grumpy about having to sit out England's crunch game: 'What made watching from the stands doubly worse was that we were surrounded by Spanish fans. One sitting behind me spent most of the match pounding a big drum and I felt like turning round and telling him to shut up.'

Scotland's Steve Archibald gets a mauling on the letters page for being 'hopeless'.

★ ★ ★

▦ A LOAD OF BALLS

■ On the day of the first-ever final, between Uruguay and Argentina in Montevideo in 1930, an intractable argument broke out when both sides demanded the use of their own ball. The fledgling FIFA competition rules had no answer to this thorny problem, until a coin toss decided in favour of the smaller Argentinian ball. Argentina were 2-1 up at half time with their ball, but the Uruguayans ignored the coin-toss outcome and used their ball for the second half, winning the game 4-2.

■ The browny-orange ball that Geoff Hurst put over the line three times (though one of his goals might have been on the line!) in the 1966 final was smuggled back to Germany by striker Helmut Haller. He returned it 30 years later and presented it to Geoff Hurst, conceding that as Hurst had scored a hat-trick in the game it was rightfully his.

■ In 1970, adidas introduced the Telstar ball – a design using a truncated icosahedron, consisting of 12 black pentagonal and 20 white hexagonal panels. It was designed with black and white television in mind.

■ The adidas Tango was introduced in 1978 and was used as the basic design for 20 years. Made of real leather and coated with waterproof Durlast, it remains a design classic. There was the odd tweak in design as a nod to host countries and new man-made materials were adopted, with the last leather ball, Tango España, appearing in 1982. This was followed by the Azteca 86, Etrusco Unico 90, Questra 94 and Tricolore 98.

■ As we entered the 21st century, adidas introduced a new design for the Korea/Japan tournament, the Fevernova. It included a foam layer with tiny gas-filled balloons imbedded in a syntactic foam, and was not popular with goalkeepers due to its lightness and unpredictable movement through the air. 'A ridiculous kiddy's bouncing ball,' was the verdict of Italian keeper Gianluigi Buffon. The shapes on the side were golden orbs sporting red flames in the motif of a *shuriken* (a Japanese hidden weapon known as a throwing star). Apparently.

■ For the 2006 tournament in Germany, adidas produced the Teamgeist (German for 'team spirit') based on four 'propeller' shapes. Each match ball was personalised with the name of the stadium, teams, date and kick-off time of each individual game. It was designed to be 'rounder', with fewer seams than the 32-panel ball, rewarding more skilful players.

Ball ten times smaller than depicted. Jermain Defoe shown actual size.

■ For the South African tournament in 2010, adidas introduced the Jabulani ('to celebrate' in isiZulu). Eleven different colours appear on the ball, representing the 11 players in every team, the 11 official languages of South Africa and the 11 South African communities. This ball's design feature will be a 'Grip'n'Groove' profile allowing for an exceptionally stable flight and perfect grip under all conditions. With eight, thermally bonded, spherically moulded, 3-D panels, the ball is perfectly round. Even more rounder than the last one.

★ ★ ★

⠿ VITAL PUB INFO
TO FOSTER FRIENDLY RELATIONS WITH FANS OF

AUSTRALIA

Fanspotter's guide
Surfboard, barbecue, tinnie or six, yellow shirt with green trim.

Conversation starter
The duck-billed platypus is an egg-laying mammal. In prehistoric times, giant kangaroos, lion-like marsupials and wombats the size of hippopotami were native to Oz. So what's all that about then, mate?

Accentuate the positive
The Socceroos coped easily in qualification, having quit the Oceania Football Confederation (OFC) and joined the Asian Football Confederation (AFC) in search of higher-class opposition.

Skirt expertly around the negative
They were unlucky to lose to a last-minute penalty against eventual champions Italy last time around in one of the matches of the finals.

Form guide
Beat Japan at home and drew away in qualifying, but will need to step up a gear to come through a competitive Group D which also features Germany, Serbia and Ghana.

Four to watch
Everton's Tim Cahill was top scorer in qualifying, he's an attacking midfielder with real Premier League class; while former Everton team-mate

Tim Cahill was grateful for the push from a Japanese defender during their June 2009 World Cup qualifier.

Lucas Neill adds bite at the back. Elsewhere in Lancashire, Blackburn supply defensive midfielder Brett Emerton and Vince Grella – the latter a hot tip for big things.

Simply the best... ever

Rolf Harris is officially the most popular artist in the world. For onfield artistry, Harry Kewell was fantastic on his day – and Brit fans may be surprised to realise he's still playing for Galatasaray, and capable of magic in South Africa.

Useful Aussie phrases

Thet Timmy Cahill – wad African jane yuss! – That Timmy Cahill. What a fricking genius

The war kabowd? Nah made, thet zack ross the stride – The Walkabout? No mate, that's across the street.

Stucta crucket, wadd own cha? – Stick to cricket, why don't you? (to be delivered after the inevitable first-round knockout)

(With thanks to Afferbeck Lauder and his wonderful *Let Stalk Strine*)

Chat-up line

It really is an honour and a pleasure to meet you, Miss Minogue...

This one's on me

VB is the biggie Down Under, not Castlemaine or Foster's.

Inside line on Australian culture

BRET: When I first met you, you tried to get me deported because you thought I was Australian.

JEMAINE: That was a misunderstanding. You were wearing a vest top.

(*Flight of the Conchords*, 2009)

Common ground

'Aussies are big and empty. Just like their country,' Sir Ian Botham.

★ ★ ★

▦ 'HILARIOUS' NAMES

■ Alex Thepot (pronounced 'Alex Teapot') – Goalkeeper, France, 1930, 1934
■ Jakob Bender – Goalkeeper, Germany, 1934
■ Willy Busch – Defender, Germany, 1934 (Germany 1934, prolifically ridiculously named team)
■ Hilario – Defender, Spain, 1934

Jose Ufarte (centre) laughs hysterically at hearing the latest joke about his name.

■ Knut Kroon – Striker, Sweden, 1934
■ Kick Smit – Striker, Netherlands, 1934, 1938
■ Walter Dick – Striker, USA, 1934
■ Tim – Striker, Brazil, 1938
■ Philibert Smellincx – Defender, Belgium, 1938
■ Dick Been – Defender, Netherlands, 1938
■ Antonio Valencia – Midfield, Bolivia, 1950
■ Hippolyte Van Den Bosch – Striker, Belgium, 1954
■ Jose Ufarte – Midfielder, Spain, 1966
■ Dominique Dropsy – Goalkeeper, France, 1978
■ Danny Boffin – Midfielder, Belgium, 1994, 1998, 2002
■ Stefan Kuntz – Striker, Germany, 1994
■ Dunga – Defender, Brazil, 1998
■ Francisco Arce – Defender, Paraguay, 1998, 2002
■ Kaká – Midfielder, Brazil, 2002, 2006
■ Nicky Butt – Midfielder, England, 2002
■ Quim – Goalkeeper, Portugal, 2006

★ ★ ★

▓ WHATEVER HAPPENED TO THE HEROES?

Karl-Heinz Schnellinger • West Germany 1958, 1962, 1966, 1970

One of a new breed of *libero* defenders whose aim wasn't simply to stop others playing. 'The Volkswagen' figured prominently in FC Köln's German Championship victory of 1962, when he was also domestic Player of the Year and a member of the 1962 World Cup All-Star XI. He was a shoo-in for the West German team in 1966, although by that time he had shocked his countrymen with a trailblazing move to Italy – well, what would you do if pneumatic actress Gina Lollobrigida had called you 'the handsomest man in football'? – plying his trade for AC Mantova ('Little Brazil') and AS Roma before revelling in nine glorious seasons with AC Milan right up until 1975. Still lives and works as a PR executive in Milan.

Uwe Seeler • West Germany 1958, 1962, 1966, 1970

A hugely popular, modest man, Uns Uwe ('Our Uwe') played in the same World Cup finals as Pelé: 1958, '62, '66 and '70. The legendary one-club striker followed his father into the Hamburg SV team, staying loyal to the club from 1953-72 while scoring a German record of 509 goals in all competitions. He ran a successful sportswear business post-football and remains a German icon thanks to *Kicker* magazine's 'Photo of the Century', which shows him devastated at the final whistle in 1966.

Mark Viduka • Australia 2006

Born in Croatia and raised in Australia to play for the Melbourne Knights, 'The Duke' returned to Croatia Zagreb in 1995, aged just 19, at the request of Croatian President Franjo Tudjman. Three league titles later, fans still barracked him as 'the president's man': cue an equally successful £3.5 million switch to Celtic. More recently, Australian fans have doubted Viduka's commitment to their cause, though he played a huge part at the 2006 World Cup, most memorably leading the line against eventual champions Italy. Powerful on the ball and in the air, strike rates of 37 goals in 48 matches (Celtic); 72 in 166 (Leeds); and even 42 in 99 (Middlesbrough) say it all. A free agent post-Newcastle, he's now rumoured to be heading back to Oz. Is it too late for the big man to heed the call of Socceroos boss Pim Verbeek?

★ ★ ★

▦ THE TALKSPORT CLASS OF 2006

1 Gianluigi Buffon • Italy Buffon, the athletic offspring of a discus-throwing mother and weightlifting father, was probably the best goalkeeper in the world in 2006. He kept five clean sheets on the way to Italy's triumph in the final. Then he did finally concede a couple, but it was from a Cristian Zaccardo own goal and a penalty from Zinédine Zidane.

2 Lilian Thuram • France Persuaded to come out of retirement for 2006, France's most-capped player had an excellent tournament, making it all the way to the final. He then retired for good, having discovered that he had the same heart condition that caused the death of his brother. This didn't stop him breaking France's all-time appearance record, however.

3 Philipp Lahm • Germany One of the world's greatest full-backs, Lahm got Germany's tournament off on the right note scoring a superb opening goal against Costa Rica. This goal, cutting in from the left and shooting with his right, was his trademark strike as Lahm is right footed, but plays at left-back.

4 Fabio Cannavaro • Italy A superb centre-half and captain who played every minute of every match, and lifted the World Cup the same night he won his hundredth cap. Cannavaro was at the heart of a miserly defence that conceded just two goals in the whole tournament.

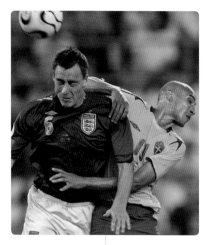

JT experiences a right pain in the neck while impersonating a young Prince Charles.

5 John Terry • England The big centre-half was an inspirational skipper and was the only England player named in the FIFA All-Star XI. His finest moment came with a face-saving overhead clearance off the line against Trinidad & Tobago.

6 Michael Ballack • Germany Missed the first game of the tournament with an injury, but recovered to play a huge part in the host nation's journey to the semi-finals. He played a captain's role, twice being named Man of the Match and making it into the FIFA All-Star team.

7 Luís Figo • Portugal The captain of Portugal's Golden Generation who inspired their best World Cup showing since the days of Eusebio. Figo retired from international football after Portugal lost to Greece in the Euro 2004 final, but, thankfully for Portugal, reversed this decision in time for Germany 2006.

8 Zinédine Zidane • France After a disappointing 2002 tournament, the midfield genius was (yet another player) persuaded out of retirement to lead France all the way to the World Cup final. Awarded the best player of the tournament gong (before that headbutt), Zidane's converted penalty against Italy saw him join an exclusive club of players who had scored in two finals along with Pelé, Paul Breitner and Vavá.

9 Hernán Crespo • Argentina An exciting striker who scored three goals before Argentina's quarter-final exit, including one in the 6-0 demolition of Serbia & Montenegro. This was enough to see the former Chelsea player gain a Silver Shoe award.

10 Miroslav Klose • Germany In 2001, Polish coach Jerzy Engel travelled to Germany and pleaded with Klose to choose Poland (the country of his birth) over Germany to no avail. Poland's loss has definitely been Germany's gain and the clinical striker won the Golden Boot, scoring five goals (matching his tally in 2002).

11 Zé Roberto • Brazil A highly talented left-sided midfielder who put in a fine performance to get Brazil past Ghana in the second round, the former Bayern Munich player is deeply religious and intends to become a pastor when he retires.

★ ★ ★

VITAL PUB INFO

TO FOSTER FRIENDLY RELATIONS WITH FANS OF

SERBIA

Fanspotter's guide

Red shirts with white trim. We wonder what Gok Wan would have to say about the red tops, blue shorts and white socks combo? And we wonder what people down the boozer will make of traditional Serbian celebrations, which involve a trumpet orchestra, women doing a hip-shaking belly dance on the table-top, while men kneel in front of them and well-wishers smash glasses.

Conversation starter

By this time, kneeling in front of your new, wiggling Serbian acquaintance, there'll be little need for a conversation starter. Let's just hope Serbia keep winning!

Accentuate the positive

Independent only since 2006, FIFA has let Serbia inherit Yugoslavia's World Cup record of 11 finals and two fourth places (1930 and 1962).

Skirt expertly around the negative

Heck, it sounds better than played 3, lost 3; goals for 2, goals against 10.

Form guide

Any team that can win their qualifying group ahead of France needs to be taken deadly seriously.

Two to watch

Unknown in Serbia until his national call-up in 2007, Standard Liege's Milan Jovanovic is on fire – a big, ebullient character. Radosav Petrovic of Partizan Belgrade is another to keep your eye on.

Simply the best... ever

Red Star Belgrade's Dragan Dzajic was one of the deadliest left-wingers in football history, playing for Yugoslavia between 1964 and 1978.

Useful Serbo-Croat phrases

Volim te svim srcem – I love you with all my heart.

Volim sarma svim srcem – I am equally fond of minced beef/pork with rice enveloped in pickled cabbage or vine leaves.

This is Serbian striker Marko Pantelic, captured just as he discovered how his name is pronounced in Doncaster. Obviously, he's never been there before.

Chat-up line

Excuse me, miss. Could you tell me how to pronounce the name of your star striker, Pantelic?

This one's on me

Serban beer (or 'pivo') tends not to be exported. Get your new Serbian mates a pint of cooking lager and a *slivovica* (plum brandy) chaser. But if in Serbia don't drink inside a football ground: President Boris Tadic was fined €400 for uncorking a bottle of champagne to celebrate their victory over Romania that guaranteed qualification to the 2010 finals.

Inside line on Serbian culture

Serbia is the world's largest raspberry exporter. If you eat a raspberry, there's a one in three chance that it's Serbian.

Common ground

They think of coach Raddy Andic as a Serbian flagwaver, famously bossing Barcelona, Real Madrid and and Atlético Madrid. We still think of him as a useful up-and-downer for Luton Town in the early 1980s.

★ ★ ★

▦ WHAT DID YOU DO DURING THE WORLD CUP, DADDY?

George Best, Northern Ireland

Best won 37 caps, scoring nine goals, but his career fell through the gaps between Northern Ireland's three tournaments in 1958, 1982 and 1986. Unfortunate for Best, and perhaps even more unfortunate for the World Cup. When Northern Ireland met the Netherlands in Rotterdam in a qualifier for the 1978 World Cup, Best kept on drifting out of position so that he could directly take on Johan Cruyff, who was widely regarded as the world's best player at the time. It is said that Billy Bingham considered taking Best to the 1982 World Cup, but let his head rule his heart and decided against taking the troubled 36-year-old to Spain. As they say in Belfast: 'Maradona good, Pelé better, George Best.'

Ryan Giggs, Wales

The Manchester United winger with an unrivalled haul of winners' medals represented England at schoolboy level but was not eligible for England, where the left side of midfield has so often been a weak link during his career. He has stated that he would have chosen Wales regardless, though he also qualified to play for Sierra Leone. During Giggs' international career from 1991 to 2007, the nearest Wales came to World Cup qualification was for USA 94, but a missed penalty in their final game against Romania wrecked their chances. He won 64 caps, scoring 12 goals.

Jim Baxter, Scotland

Regarded as one of Scotland's most talented players, Baxter's 34 caps were earned during Scotland's 16-year absence from the World Cup finals between 1958 and 1974. The nearest Baxter came to a finals tournament was in 1962 when Scotland finished joint top of their group, but then lost

Helping Scotland to beat the World Champions, Slim Jim's unorthodox jumping style was occasionally compared to that of a man with an excessively ironed shirt.

a play-off to Czechoslovakia. Baxter suffered a broken leg at the time Scotland were attempting to qualify for 1966 and they came second behind Italy. He did star in the side that beat England 3-2 at Wembley in 1967, however, which many Scots regarded as a battle for the world title!

Ian Rush, Wales

Liverpool's goal machine never made it to the ultimate stage. Despite several near misses Wales have made it to the World Cup only once and that was in 1958, three years before Rush was born. Wales went close in 1982, 1986 and 1994, but Rush, who bagged an impressive 28 goals in 73 games (including winners against Germany and Italy), was destined never to grace a final tournament.

Ray Clemence, England

Failure by England to qualify for the 1974 and 1978 World Cups denied Clemence an appearance in the finals at a time when he was alternating with Peter Shilton as England's number one. By the time England qualified for Spain in 1982, Shilton had made the yellow jersey his own. So, despite having the No 1 shirt, Clemence was destined to spend the entire tournament on the bench, and not one of his 61 caps was won in the finals of a World Cup. The same fate befell his long-term Liverpool team-mate Emlyn Hughes, who won 62 caps.

Alfredo Di Stefano, Argentina

One of the greatest players in the history of the game, Di Stefano somehow contrived to miss four different tournaments. In 1950, Argentina did not enter; in 1954, Argentina didn't enter again, but by now Di Stefano had moved on to Colombia and upset FIFA by playing for them. By 1958, he was playing for Real Madrid and had Spanish citizenship. Although he played in

Di Stefano suddenly discovers that he's less likely than Ronnie Corbett to appear in a World Cup final.

qualifying games for Spain, they didn't make it to Sweden. Finally, in 1962, Di Stefano helped Spain qualify for Chile, but was injured shortly before the tournament began and missed out once again.

Bernd Schuster, West Germany

Schuster played in two of West Germany's games in Euro 80 in Italy, including the final when they achieved a 2-1 victory over Belgium. He impressed enough to win the Silver Ball Trophy, awarded to the second-best player in the tournament, but then brought a halt to his international career at the tender age of 24. He announced his retirement from international football having fallen out with the German Football Association, manager Jupp Derwall, and a couple of team-mates. He went on to star for Barcelona and Real Madrid, but never played for his country again.

Eric Cantona, France

Although Cantona made his debut for France in 1987, he was soon banned from international football for observing of the French coach Henri Michel: 'I am not far from thinking that he is a bag of shit.' France failed to qualify for the 1990 and 1994 World Cups, and Cantona was again unavailable in 1995 after serving a ban for attacking a fan at Selhurst Park. By the time the 1998 World Cup in France came round, Zinédine Zidane had taken on the role of play-maker for les Bleus, and Cantona had retired from the game.

Abédi ('Pelé') Ayew, Ghana

The hugely talented Ghanaian midfielder was widely considered to be one of the greatest African footballers in history, and was one of the first to play in Europe, joining Marseille at the start of their highly successful spell in the 1990s. His international career spanned 16 years, and Ayew scored 33 goals in 73 appearances, but Ghana never reached a World Cup during this time. Abédi has recently acquired a stain on his character, being involved in a play-off bribery scandal that saw his team Nania FC beat Okwawu United 31-0, though he subsequently had his penalty quashed.

Duncan Edwards, England

Tragically, we'll never know what the brilliant young Edwards would have achieved in World Cup tournaments. He was certainly assured of his place in the England squad for 1958 and, judging by the many accolades he picked up in his short career, probably for many years after that. He was seriously injured in the plane crash at Munich-Riem Airport on 6 February 1958, and died 15 days later. Sir Bobby Charlton has said of him that he was: 'Simply the greatest footballer of all time.'

▦ CHEAT! CHEAT! CHEAT!

■ In 1989, Chilean goalkeeper Roberto Rojas was responsible for some of the finest – and oddest – theatrics in the history of the World Cup. With his country losing to Brazil in a qualifying match and subsequently facing elimination from the 1990 tournament, Rojas decided it was up to him to get the game abandoned. So, he did what any clear-thinking, practical human being would do, and sliced his face open with a concealed razor blade, in attempt to make it look like he'd been hit by a firework. This foolproof plan was only scuppered due to the fact that several high-resolution television cameras were trained on him at the time. Rojas was promptly banned from football for life.

■ Mexico were banned from the 1990 World Cup because of irregularities in an international youth tournament when it was discovered that they had falsified the ages of three players.

■ In 1954, West German coach Sepp Herberger fielded a team packed with reserves against Hungary, aiming to lose and secure an easier quarter-final tie. They lost, and so were able to progress to the final: winning 7-2 against Turkey, 2-0 against Yugoslavia and 6-1 against Austria.

■ Argentina 6 Peru 0, 1978. Hosts Argentina needed to beat Peru by at least four to stay in the tournament...

★ ★ ★

▦ VITAL PUB INFO
TO FOSTER FRIENDLY RELATIONS WITH FANS OF

GHANA

Fanspotter's guide

Look out for the all-white kit with black piping, and women wearing colourful swathes of printed fabric.

Conversation starter

People from the Ivory Goast are called Ivorians. So when Ghana was called the Gold Coast, what were Ghanaians known as?

Accentuate the positive

The Black Satellites won the Under-20 World Cup in 2009, beating Brazil in the final despite going down to ten men.

Skirt expertly around the negative

Once rated as high as No 14 in the FIFA rankings back in 2008, the Black Stars are now well down in the 30s.

Form guide

Ranked sixth in Africa, a draw with Mali clinched qualification for Ghana. Their young side got to the final of the African Cup of Nations for the first time since 1992, beating Nigeria in the semi-finals and keeping their fifth successive clean sheet.

Two to watch

Skipper and Bologna midfielder Stephen Appiah is a match-winner, if only he can stay fit. Matthew Amoah (NAC Breda) was top scorer in qualifying, as pivotal up front as he was in 2006.

Simply the best... ever

Abédi Pelé was African Footballer of the Year in 1991, 1992 and 1993. The only player to run him close was ex-Leeds powerhouse Tony Yeboah – but sadly the two fell out and never played together to their potential.

Useful Twi phrases

Etisen – a cunning mixture of 'hello' and 'how are you?'.

Mie nu-baaku – 2-1 (useful in case it's 2-1 and someone asks you the score).

Chat-up line

Love of the family and respect for the elderly are both important to traditional Ghanaians. For Ghana's big match, take your dad down the juicer as a useful bargaining tool.

This one's on me

Make mine a palm wine – and shall we go on for a *shito* (it's a peppery veg stew made with powdered shrimp and powdered herring)?

Inside line on Ghanaian culture

Sankofa is a splendid Ghanaian principle that suggests we must return to our roots in order to move forward – 'it is not taboo to go back and fetch what you forgot.' Especially if it's your pooch down the juicer.

Common ground

Michael Essien and John Pantsil currently play in London, for Chelsea and Fulham. Bill Garner used to play for Chelsea and Southend.

★ ★ ★

⠿ IT'S ALL GONE OFF
(PART TWO) THE PLAYERS

Harald Schumacher • Germany 1982, 1986

In the 1982 finals, German goalkeeper 'Toni' Schumacher took out French forward Patrick Battiston, running at him full-on and sending him head over heels with a full body check. Battiston was prone, unmoving on the pitch and players reacted as if he were dead. In World Cup 1986, Battiston proclaimed the incident was 'forgiven and forgotten', despite those damaged vertebrae and two missing teeth – though, as a footnote, he did add that he wouldn't get within 40 yards of him on the pitch. Eventually, Schu blew his hard-man image by grassing up German team-mates for substance abuse, and later acted as best man at Battiston's wedding.

Nobby Stiles • England 1966

Known as the 'Toothless Tiger' for his unnerving habit of removing his dentures before battle, Nobby is remembered today almost exclusively for his late, mis-timed and uncompromising tackles; but he could play a bit, too. 'Nobby was a great reader of the game,' says United team-mate Paddy Crerand. 'Height didn't matter, he was a great defender. I always thought when he played he was one of the most important players and you wanted him in your team. He was a great driving force.' Playing in front of the back four for England in 1966, he battled toe-to-toe with Argentina and man-marked Eusebio out of the Portugal semi, having committed a particularly horrific tackle against France – so bad that FA bigwigs actually brought pressure on Ramsey to drop Stiles for the final. But Alf stayed loyal. And Nobby provided the 35-yard pass for Hunt to pull back for Hurst's third.

Andoni Goikoetxea • Spain 1986

During his 12 years at centre-back for Athletic Bilbao, the Basque Goikoetxea helped his club to the Spanish Liga in 1983, followed the next year by the League and Cup double. But it was a different kind of trophy that cemented his reputation as football's hardest case. In a glass display cabinet in his living room, the so-called 'Butcher of Bilbao' kept the boot with which he had laid waste to Maradona's ankle ligaments with a scything tackle from behind that put Barça's Catalan poster boy out of the game for a year.

Claudio Gentile • Italy 1978, 1982

There were a few outraged fans who rated Italian team-mate Marco Tardelli harder than Gentile during their reign of terror in the 1980s – Jimmy Greaves reckoned Tardelli was 'responsible for more scar tissue than the surgeons at Harefield Hospital' – but we'll stick with the granite-faced man-marker from Libya. Others dared to whisper that Giuseppe Bergomi was the man to fear in Italy's midfield, just because he had the blank-eyed stare of a serial killer. But only our man Gentile (it's Italian for 'nice') kicked, harassed and manhandled Maradona and then Zico out of the 1982 World Cup, and went on to lift the trophy with his chilling one-liner still ringing in fans' ears: 'Football is not for ballerinas.'

Antonio Rattin • Argentina 1962, 1966

One of Argentina's most popular players of all time, Rattin was a born leader – a super-fit, muscular hustler, a magnet for the ball and an intimidating presence in the midfield. If he'd been playing for England in that quarter-final back in 1966, we'd probably have taken him to our hearts for arguing the toss with the German ref, getting sent off in spurious circumstances for 'violence of the tongue' (despite the official speaking no Spanish and Rattin no German), steadfastly refusing to leave the field in the face of an apparent conspiracy, and sparking a 20-minute walkout by his team-mates. But lordy, we could have no truck with what happened next. On his long, lonely walk around the pitch, Rattin dared to crumple a corner flag as he passed by. A flag which just happened to sport a Union Jack. Then he sat on the red carpet reserved only for the feet of the beloved Queen.

The 'Animal' (Copyright © Sir Alf Ramsey).

★ ★ ★

▦ *SCORCHER* EXCUSES

How did *Scorcher* comic cope when the worlds of fact and fiction collided? What would their made-up characters do when the real World Cup infringed on their imaginary existence? Here are the reasons why not a single one of the regular comic strip heroes played in, or even mentioned, the World Cup in June 1974:

■ **Nipper** Nipper Lawrence and his pal and Blackport Rovers team-mate Mike Bateson accepted jobs as sports instructors at Paradise Pines boys' camp in Wales.

■ **Jack & Jimmy** Jack and Jimmy Chelsey of Castleburn City were both picked to represent the Football League on a continental tour. Their tracksuits have 'England' on the back.

■ **Billy's Boots** Despite being pretty hopeless whenever his magic boots had been slung into a skip or a river by a bully, or sold in a jumble sale by his gran, Billy Dane was selected by Southern Schools to go on a tour of Denmark and Norway.

■ **Hot Shot Hamish** Despite having a shot that could, and did, knock over a factory chimney, Hamish Balfour was mysteriously left out of the Scottish World Cup squad. He spent a week at his daddy's rain-swept Hebridean island home and then went on a three-game tour of France with Princes Park.

■ **The Boy in the Velvet Mask** Alan Hemmings, Lynchester United's mysterious masked goalkeeper, spent his close season running on the moors and trying to escape a photographer determined to reveal his true identity.

■ **Lags Eleven** The convicts' football team somehow managed to blag a tour of South America, where they take on a side called the Jinka Javelins.

■ **Alf's Albion** Young millionaire Alf Littlegood takes his Alfchurch Albion side on his private aircraft carrier (with football pitch) to the tiny republic of San Barino for a friendly.

■ **Bobby of the Blues** Bobby Booth travels with Everpool City for a South American tour.

★ ★ ★

⠿ TALKING A GOOD GAME

We shall win the World Cup.

Alf Ramsey, October 1963, upon his appointment as England manager

▦ CLUBS BACKING ENGLAND FOR THE WORLD CUP

For England's previous World Cup campaigns, this list shows which clubs have provided the most players to the national cause. Of the 2009-10 Premiership teams, only Hull City and Wigan Athletic have never provided a player for England's World Cup squad. The list in full is:

- Manchester United – 31
- Tottenham Hotspur – 26
- Liverpool – 22
- Arsenal – 17
- Chelsea – 15
- West Ham United – 13
- Wolverhampton Wanderers – 12
- Leeds United – 11
- Everton – 9
- Newcastle United, West Bromwich Albion – 8
- Blackpool, Fulham – 6
- Aston Villa, Blackburn Rovers, Manchester City, Middlesbrough, Nottingham Forest – 5
- Ipswich Town, Rangers, Sheffield Wednesday, Southampton 4
- Bolton Wanderers, Huddersfield Town, Preston North End, Sheffield United – 3
- AC Milan, Bayern Munich, Birmingham City, Burnley, Derby County, Leicester City, Portsmouth, Queens Park Rangers, Sunderland – 2
- Brighton & Hove Albion, FC Cologne, Inter Milan, Luton Town, Marseille, Norwich City, Real Madrid, Stoke City, Watford – 1

Hands up who worked out that Gerry Hitchens was Inter's sole contribution to England's World Cup efforts? Here he puts one past the Hearts keeper.

▓ VITAL PUB INFO
TO FOSTER FRIENDLY RELATIONS WITH FANS OF

THE NETHERLANDS

Fanspotter's guide
Look like they've just been Tangoed.

Conversation starter
Amsterdam has over a million bicycles, but only 700,000 human citizens. Are they breeding? Are they planning a takeover? Don't you smell a horror film in the making...

The Dutch tourist board could never understand why Amsterdam was so popular with visitors.

Accentuate the positive
Dutch soccer expert David Winner explains why the national team can be so wonderful to watch in his classic *Brilliant Orange* (Bloomsbury, 2000). Space is precious in tiny, densely populated Netherlands, leading to brilliant, abstract use of the stuff, as well as an abnormal 3D spacial appreciation. This explains how the Dutch came to play Total Football – and how they come to build a Total Airport such as Schiphol, constructed on the site of a famous naval battle. It's superbly functional, rational and pragmatic.

Skirt expertly around the negative
Winner concludes that the Dutch aren't efficient in the German sense. They like things level and flat. They don't like peaks in landscape or performance.

Better to be universally recognised as the best team than actually win, viz. the major tournaments of 1974, 78, 98 and 2000.

Form guide

Came through the qualifiers with eight straight wins, winning the group by 14 points from Norway and Scotland. In history, only eventual winners Brazil (1970) and West Germany (1982) have managed this feat. Trouble is, Spain also pulled it off this time around – and, unlike the Netherlands, have gone on to do slightly more than scrape three uninspiring, scoreless friendly draws against Australia, Italy and Paraguay.

Five to watch

Brit fans will be familiar with Arjen Robben, Robin van Persie and Dirk Kuyt, but we don't half like the look of the former Ajax kids Rafael van der Vaart and Wesley Sneijder, the midfield pairing reunited briefly at Real Madrid before Wes moved on to Inter.

Simply the best... ever

Johan Cruyff. But let's spare a thought for Gullit, Van Basten, Neeskens...

Useful Dutch phrases

Ruud van Nistelrooy loopt in een bar. De barman vragen onmiddellijk zijn gezicht lengte. – Ruud van Nistelrooy walks into a bar. The barman immediately questions his facial length.

Wat is er gebeurd met Jordi Cruyff? – Whatever happened to Jordi Cruyff?

Is mijn accent zo overtuigend als die van Steve McClaren? – Is my accent as convincing as that of Steve McClaren?

Chat-up line

Did you know, Martin Jol has brothers named 'Cock' and 'Dick'. I'm part of his extended family...

This one's on me

Dick Advocaat.

Inside line on Dutch culture

There is a famous houseboat in Amsterdam called *Poezenboot*, which acts a home for stray cats. It began life in 1966 when a feline philanthropist (or 'feline-thropist', if you like) named Henriette van Weelde took pity on a few vagrant kittens and bought them their own floating home. The boat is now one of the most famous cat sanctuaries in the world, and attracts visitors from all over the world. However, the visitors may just be swarming in to laugh openly at the hordes of stoned English kids nearby, all rubbing their bloodshot eyes and whispering to each other, 'Hey man, I swear that boat was full of cats.'

Common ground

Christmas in the Netherlands is a bizarre affair. Rather than our own good-natured, ruddy-faced Santa Claus, Dutch children are warned to expect a visit from 'Sinterklaas': a sociopathic bearded loon, who seeks out the 'naughty' kids, thrashes them with willow branches and then sends them to Spain in a sack. Manchester United insiders have suggested that this legend was the inspiration behind Sir Alex's treatment of Ruud van Nistelrooy in 2006!

★ ★ ★

▦ WORLD CUP SONGS
ITALY 1990

Englandneworder • 'World In Motion'

(Number 1)

This may be a World Cup classic and New Order's only number one, but in reality it's far from one of their best. 'We sing E for England' was an audacious druggy smuggling job in the coda, but Keith Allen's lyrics are

Lily Allen's dad gets an idea for a career after his acting work has dried up. Hmm... wonder what our Lily's up to?

generally clunky, and hit rock bottom in the John Barnes rap: 'Catch me if you can / 'cos I'm the England man / And what you're looking for / Is the master plan.' Allen hogged the rap himself on the flipside, which quite probably served him right.

This time around, the Scotland World Cup Squad was led into battle by Fish out of Marillion, whose 'Say It With Pride' could have been so much better if he'd invited along Big Country with their weird bagpipe guitars. 'Put 'Em Under Pressure' was the official Republic of Ireland Football Squad effort, a sampladelic singalong featuring chunks of 'Wor' Jackie Charlton getting inspirational, other chunks of 'Olé Olé Olé' and revenge chunks of 'Ally's Tartan Army' – which was originally set to the tune of 'God Save Ireland'! It was all Larry Mullen Jr out of U2's fault.

Pavarotti's 'Nessun Dorma' was the BBC's memorable theme tune, now forever associated with missed penalties. But for anyone who was camped out in the big-screen boozer in the baggietastic summer of '90, soundtrack domination was shared by New Order, Primal Scream's 'Loaded' and 'Step On' by the Happy Mondays. And we're not twisting your melon, man.

★ ★ ★

▦ WHAT THE PAPERS SAY
1986 WORLD CUP

Shoot! covered the Mexico World Cup as follows in its 19 July edition (yours for just 40p).

Who else but Diego Maradona is on the front cover, hoisted shoulder high and holding aloft the World Cup next to the headline, 'KING of the WORLD'.

Among the features was an article entitled 'Argentina's All-Star Cast – They're Not a One Man Band', which is not very convincing, while in 'Banks or Shilton – Who is the Greatest?' Bob Wilson is the judge and he bottles it, giving them both 87 points out of 100. 'The Stunners' looks at the biggest wins of the tournament: USSR beat Hungary 6-0, Denmark beat Uruguay 6-1, Spain beat Denmark 5-1. 'The Guilty Men' – Scotland's excursion among the elite was all too predictable and all too brief…

The cartoon 'Laughline' showed a circus clown and someone commenting: 'Just back from Mexico – he was one of the refs.' The feature ROBBED! takes up the theme, concentrating on the tournament's controversial decisions: Maradona's Hand of God goal; Iraq's goal against Paraguay scored one second after the ref's half-time whistle; and Spain's goal that had clearly gone over the line against Brazil. But Jimmy Greaves is there to stick up for Maradona about one of those decisions, amid the furore on the letters page: 'My first memory of him isn't that questionable first goal against England, but the brilliant second.'

Colour action of Argentina beating West Germany in the final is complemented by a 12-page colour review of the World Cup with Maradona kissing the trophy.

Finally, in the 'Focus On' section, Michael Laudrup reveals the following about his life: Home: La Colline, a penthouse apartment in the hills near Turin; Car: Fiat Uno; Football Hero: Johan Cryuff; Hobbies: Playing chess and tennis; Favourite Musicians: Wham, ELO and Duran Duran.

★ ★ ★

MASCOTS

World Cup Willie • England 1966

The first FIFA-sanctioned World Cup mascot was a tubby lion wearing a Union Jack waistcoat (although it should really have been the flag of St George, being England's tournament and not Britain's). Willie appeared in a cartoon strip in *TV Comic* and Lonnie Donegan wrote a song about him:

Dressed in red, white and blue, he's World Cup Willie
We all love him too, World Cup Willie
He's tough as a lion and never will give up
That's why Willie is favourite for the Cup

Not as good as 'Rock Island Line', admittedly. Willie was last seen in the High Court in 2007 when a company tried to register his image as a trademark and the FA, not surprisingly, objected.

Juanito • Mexico 1970

A little boy wearing the Mexico kit and a huge sombrero with 'Mexico 70' written on it. Not the most imaginative, but it worked.

Tip and Tap • West Germany 1974

Two incredibly happy cartoon boys, a short dark one and a tall blond one. Like Ant and Dec, they worked best as a pair.

Gauchito • Argentina 1978

A little boy dressed in traditional Gaucho costume, the horseman of the Pampas. Wearing a broad beaming smile that did nothing to alert the world to the excesses of a military junta and 30,000 'disappeared'.

Naranjito • Spain 1982

After eight years of boy mascots, it was time to bring on the fruit and veg. Naranjito was a big, round, lovable orange with an imbecilic smile.

Pique • Mexico 1986

The Jalapeno pepper, a cornerstone of Mexican cuisine – in a sombrero. His name derived from *picante*, the Spanish for spicy peppers and sauces.

Ciao • Italy 1990

Something of a departure – a footballer seemingly made of red, white and green Lego bricks with a football for a head.

Striker • USA 1994

Swerving the more obvious Bald Eagle (the one out of the *Muppet Show* would have done nicely) the US opted for a cartoon pup.

Footix • France 1998

Again, not much time was wasted at the design and concept stage – a Cockerel in France's colours that looked like a not too distant relative of Woody Woodpecker.

Ato, Kaz and Nik • Japan/South Korea 2002

Mascots for a new millennium, known collectively as the Spheriks, these semi-translucent CGI figures lived in the 'Atmozone' and played 'Atmoball'. Ato (the tallest one) was the coach while Kaz and Nik were players, apparently.

Nobody ever took responsibility for the toxic spill at the Teletubbies' house.

Goleo VI and his assistant Pille • Germany 2006

Goleo VI was the rather wild-eyed lion mascot for the Germany 2006 World Cup. His friend was a football called Pille who had blue eyes and a wide red smile. Put them together and the overall effect was vaguely unsettling, like a strange version of *Bear in the Big Blue House*, fittingly enough as Goleo was created by the Jim Henson Company.

Goleo sparked something of a scandal across Germany, partly because a lion is an animal more associated with England or the Netherlands than Germany, and also because although he wore a German football shirt, he never wore any shorts. The Germans thought his nakedness from the waist down was distasteful, concentrating on the question: 'Why isn't this Lion wearing shorts?' rather than the more obvious: 'Why is this Lion wearing a shirt?' Either way Goleo lost the shirt off his back when the German licence-holder to produce Goleo, Bavarian toy company NICI, filed for bankruptcy just before the tournament.

Zakumi • South Africa 2010

A leopard with a green mane, so named because ZA is the international abbreviation for South Africa, and 'kumi' means ten in several African languages. FIFA describe him thus: 'a jolly, self-confident, adventurous, spontaneous, and actually quite shrewd little fellow. He loves to perform and always follows his instinct and intuition, yet sometimes has the tendency to exaggerate a bit.'

★ ★ ★

▦ TALKING A GOOD GAME

US goalkeeper Kasey Keller on the clash between Iran and the USA, France 98

I spent four years at Millwall so I'm sure that's prepared me for whatever happens on Sunday.

⠿ VITAL PUB INFO
TO FOSTER FRIENDLY RELATIONS WITH FANS OF

DENMARK

Fanspotter's guide
Look out for large blond men and, ahem, athletic Scandinavian women in red shirts.

Conversation starter
Anyone for *smørrebrød*? (Think open sandwiches, heavy on smoked and marinated fish.)

Accentuate the positive
First appeared in 1986 and showed well, building to win the 1992 Euros and climb as high as No 3 in the FIFA world rankings in the late 1990s.

Skirt expertly around the negative
But they're now back down at the wrong end of the 20s. And the skipper is sometime Newcastle flop Jon Dahl Tomasson, now of Feyenoord.

Form guide
Pipped Portugal to the automatic qualifying place in European Group 1, beating them away and drawing at home. Sweden and Hungary were decent scalps, too. But does coach Morten Olsen have enough flair and quality to mount a serious challenge?

Two to watch
Nicklas Bendtner of Arsenal was Danish Player of the Year in 2009, and is ready to step up a level of greatness, while many English fans will remember veteran Ajax winger Dennis Rommedahl from his three years at Charlton.

Simply the best... ever
'Pelé was the best in the 60s, Cruyff in the 70s, Maradona in the 80s and Laudrup in the 90s,' Franz Beckenbauer

Useful Danish phrases
Vearsco, voar er bathe vaerelset – Please, where is the bathroom?
Yeg leder efter boghandel – I'm looking for a bookshop (not to be confused with a *vaerelset* or a bog handle)

Chat-up line
You're melting my heart in the same way that global warming is affecting your homeland within the Arctic Circle.

Don't mention
1970s retro pornography.

This one's on me

A pint of Carlsberg should hit the spot, especially at around half the price Danes are used to paying at home. Best go steady on the ice-cold *akvavit*, a flavoured spirit which is 40 percent proof.

Inside line on Danish culture

The Danes pride themselves on their Viking heritage, which is rather confusingly watered down by a keen regard for politeness, punctuality and equality.

Common ground

Danish blue cheese and good old Lego; Great Dane dogs and Peter 'The Great Dane' Schmeichel.

★ ★ ★

▦ LONGEST WORLD CUP NAME

Lefter Küçükandonyadis is a Turkish goalscoring legend. Lefter bagged 423 goals for Fenerbahçe and 22 for the national side in 55 appearances, stretched between 1948 and 1963. He was the first Turkish player to move abroad, appearing for Fiorentina, Nice and AEK Athens, but it's those 613 games for Kadıköy that ensure he remains a name on Turkish fans' lips.

★ ★ ★

▦ WHATEVER HAPPENED TO THE HEROES?

Faruk Hadžibegić • Yugoslavia 1990

Faruk holds a special place in the hearts of all Yugoslav football fans – the same place as Stuart Pearce in England fans' memories, and Roberto Baggio for Italians. He missed the final, conclusive penalty in the 1990 World Cup quarter-final against Argentina. Capped 61 times, his seven best years were spent at FC Sochaux in France, where he later returned as manager before becoming Bosnia boss in 1999. More recently in charge of a string of lower-league French teams, he took control of SC Bastia in December 2009.

Roger Milla • Cameroon 1982, 1990, 1994

The African Footballer of the Century was a trailblazer, starring for Bastia, Saint-Étienne and Montpellier throughout the 1980s, going on to join the latter's coaching staff after hanging up his boots. In the 1990s, at Cameroon's national stadium in Yaoundé, the World Cup legend organised a benefit match for his country's indigenous rainforest people. Sadly, only 50 tickets were sold – to punters keen to verbally abuse the Pygmy Representative XI. So the little dudes were stranded in the stadium for the duration of the summer, and very nearly starved to death. A spokesman nevertheless defended Milla, as reported in Simon Kuper's *Football Against The Enemy*: 'They play better if they don't eat too much.'

★ ★ ★

▦ TALKING A GOOD GAME

Chris Waddle, quoted in *All Played Out,* Pete Davies (1990)

How Maradona can say it's the hand of God – it's the biggest load of crap I've ever heard. If he'd have come out after the match and said, yeah, I handled it – everybody would have thought, well at least he's honest.

⠿ TALKSPORT'S ALL-TIME WORST ENGLAND WORLD CUP XI

This is the team that was voted for by the readers of talkSPORT.net/mag, and includes players who appeared in World Cup qualifiers, as well as the finals – which may explain the number of Graham Taylor's selections in our line-up.

1 Chris Woods The Rangers keeper somehow became first choice for England in between the Shilton and Seaman eras, winning 43 caps.

2 Tony Dorigo England must have fallen on hard times, selecting an Australian left-back 15 times in the early 1990s.

3 Chris Powell England debut aged 31 in 2001, thanks to Sven, and still turning out as Leicester City's emergency left-back.

4 Danny Mills Played all five matches of England's 2002 World Cup campaign, and even got Ronaldinho red-carded – alas, all to no avail.

5 Martin Keown Offloaded to Aston Villa for just £125,000 by new Arsenal boss George Graham in 1986 – who then splashed £2 million to bring him back seven years later. He won 43 caps between 1992 and 2002.

6 Carlton Palmer As he once told *90 Minutes* magazine: 'If you want the best midfielder in the world, you want Carlton Palmer.' This was incorrect, but he still won 18 caps in the early 1990s.

7 Andy Sinton A decent winger in his days at QPR, Spurs and Sheffield Wednesday, but seldom likened to Jairzinho. He won 12 caps between 1991 and 1993 under Graham Taylor.

8 Stuart Ripley Blackburn's useful left-winger won two caps during the 1990s – four years apart.

9 Kieran Richardson Surprisingly, the Sunderland up-and-downer won eight caps (and, unbelievably, scored two goals) back in his Manchester United days.

10 Darius Vassell Euro spot-kick failure overrides all memories of a decent goal haul of six in 22 appearances. Currently with Turkish side Ankaragücü.

11 Emile Heskey With 23 goals in his first season at Liverpool, the £11 million man has now won 57 caps under four different England bosses, and is still a regular under Capello.

'Sorry, son. It's just that we realised you shouldn't have been on the pitch.'

▦ VITAL PUB INFO
TO FOSTER FRIENDLY RELATIONS WITH FANS OF

JAPAN

Ludicrous headwear sales were going through the roof, but the sales of dental floss were definitely struggling.

Fanspotter's guide

Listen out for wildly enthusiastic Far Eastern fans wearing the hallowed blue nylon of the Soccer Nippon Daihyo (literally the 'Japanese soccer representatives').

Conversation starter

Break the ice with a three-line, 17-syllable haiku about a bullet train.

Accentuate the positive

After 2002's free ride as co-hosts, the Blue Samurai were the first team to qualify for South Africa this time around...

Skirt expertly around the negative

... With a 1-0 win over mighty Uzbekistan in June 2009 – a full year before the finals. Australia, Bahrain and Qatar making up the cushiest of groups.

Form guide

Did some useful swotting by taking on South Africa in the Nelson Mandela Bay Stadium, Port Elizabeth. They drew 0-0.

Two to watch

Espanyol's former Celtic star Shunsuke Nakamura enjoys a reputation as one of the world's ultimate free-kick specialists; meanwhile fellow midfielder Gamba Osaka's Yasuhito Endo was named 2009 Asian Player of the Year.

Simply the best... ever

Hidetoshi Nakata fared well in Italian stints at Roma, Parma and Fiorentina. He ended his career on loan at Bolton in 2006, just as our Gary Lineker had played his last games for Nagoya Grampus 8 back in the early 1990s.

Useful Japanese phrases

Ganbare Igirisu! – Come on England!

Tsumero! Kezure baka yaro! – Close him down! Take him out, you idiot!

Chat-up line

Take off your shoes, bow from the waist, give a gift with both hands, sit in strict order of social rank, look her in the face for less than three seconds... and ask if it's true what they say about geisha girls. (It isn't.)

This one's on me

Go for a sushi and major on those vast tins of Japanese beer, where the whole top comes off.

Inside line on Japanese culture

Do not stick chopsticks into rice as this is only done on the altar at funerals. Do not lie down after eating or it is believed you will turn into a cow.

Common ground

The manga comic/anime cartoon/video game *Captain Tsubasa* is a cult among bedroom-reared soccer kids worldwide: think Teenage Mutant Ninja Turtles doing improbable overhead kicks.

★ ★ ★

▦ TOP TEN ENGLAND INJURIES AND ILLNESSES

1 Jimmy Greaves • England 1966

Considered by many to be the most talented goalscorer of his generation, Jimmy Greaves picked up an injury in England's final Group 1 game

Copper: 'Never mind where the Saint is sunshine. You just keep moving. Roger Hunt's dad's behind you.'

against France, gashing his right shin. As England progressed towards the final, Greaves regained his fitness, but Alf Ramsey elected to stick with a winning side; a decision that was wholly vindicated by Hurst's hat-trick in the final against West Germany. Behind-the-scenes photos and film footage of the World Cup final portray a devastated figure, and Greaves later said: 'I felt sorry for myself and sick that I was out. But I was not, and have never been, in any way bitter against Alf. He did his job and England won the trophy.'

2 Gordon Banks • Mexico 1970

On the day before England's quarter-final meeting with West Germany in Leon, Gordon Banks succumbed to 'Montezuma's Revenge' or 'dicky tum' – and spent his time between bed and bathroom. He took a fitness test on the morning of the game, but Sir Alf Ramsey judged that he wasn't his usual self and Chelsea's Peter Bonetti got the nod.

It didn't seem to matter who was in goal, as England built up a commanding 2-0 lead through Alan Mullery and Martin Peters; but then Bonetti allowed a shot from Beckenbauer under his body and the Germans were back in it. Uwe Seeler then lobbed a header over Bonetti for the equaliser and Gerd Mueller completed the job in extra time. Banks had watched the game on TV in his room and drifted off to sleep while England were two goals ahead. He was woken up by third-choice keeper Alex Stepney coming into his room and silently holding up three fingers on one hand and two on the other.

3 Kevin Keegan • Spain 1982

When Keegan was the brightest star in British football in the 1970s, England twice failed to qualify for the World Cup. When they got to Spain in 1982, Keegan's World Cup career was then further curtailed by a back injury and he managed just 26 minutes as a substitute against the host nation in the second group round. He missed a golden opportunity late in the game, sending a header wide, and the 0-0 scoreline meant that England were flying home.

4 Trevor Brooking • Spain 1982

The West Ham midfielder had a remarkably similar story to Keegan's, being robbed of World Cup opportunities by England's failure to qualify throughout the 1970s. He was also restricted to 26 minutes of the Spain game, coming on as sub at the same time as Keegan, and also missed a chance to keep England in the tournament, Luis Arconada getting down to his low shot.

5 Bryan Robson • Mexico 1986

England's talismanic captain had endured a terrible time with injuries in the season leading up to Mexico 86, but he was considered by manager Bobby Robson to be too vital to England's chances to be omitted. His right shoulder had been dislocated during the domestic season, and again during acclimatisation training in Colorado. In England's second group game, against Morocco, an innocuous-looking fall left Robson writhing in agony. Despite the special harness he was wearing, the shoulder had popped out of its socket yet again. Robson's World Cup was over and he returned to a hospital bed in England.

6 Gary Lineker • Mexico 1986

Lineker injured his wrist in a pre-World Cup friendly against Canada and, at first, it was feared broken. Happily for England's prospects, it turned out to be a bad sprain and the Everton striker, who had scored 40 goals in 1985-86, was able to play with his wrist and lower arm in a lightweight plaster. It certainly didn't seem to hamper him in any way as he notched up a fine hat-trick in the opening 34 minutes of the final group game against Poland in Monterrey.

7 David Seaman • Italy 1990

Possibly the least important England injury ever, David Seaman hurt his thumb in training just before the tournament started, but was third choice keeper behind Peter Shilton and Chris Woods. He was replaced by Chelsea's David Beasant.

8 David Beckham • Japan/South Korea 2002

When football superstar and media darling David Beckham was injured in a challenge with Argentinian Aldo Duscher in Manchester United's UEFA Champions League quarter-final game against Deportivo La Coruña a nation held its breath. The news was not good. The second metatarsal bone was broken – three months before the start of the 2002 World Cup. Beckham had virtually dragged England through qualification, and life without him was not something most fans wanted to contemplate.

A nation prayed...literally. The *Sun* newspaper used its front page to urge its readers to lay their hands on a photo of Beckham's foot and pray for a swift recovery. Under intensive treatment, England's golden boy did recover sufficiently to play in Japan, but he was never 100 percent. He did, however, gain revenge over the Argentinians – converting a penalty that secured a 1-0 win in Sapporo and helped eliminate them at the group stage.

9 Wayne Rooney • Germany 2006

The curse of the metatarsal returned when Manchester United's precocious young talent Wayne Rooney fractured the base of his fourth metatarsal in a league game against Chelsea in April. Paulo Ferreira, Chelsea's Portuguese full-back, appeared to have struck the first blow of the 2006 World Cup. With the help of the best technology available to man, including the use of an oxygen tent, Rooney staged a miraculous recovery. But, like Beckham before him, he appeared to be short of match fitness. He missed the first game against Paraguay; came on as sub against Trinidad & Tobago; started but was substituted against Sweden; played the whole game against Ecuador in the second round; and then exited the World Cup ignominiously, being dismissed after 62 minutes of the quarter-final against Portugal after stamping on Ricardo Carvalho and clashing with Cristiano Ronaldo. Be careful what you wish for...

10 Michael Owen • Germany 2006

Less than a minute into England's last group game against Sweden in Cologne, the injury-plagued Owen turned awkwardly and his knee collapsed under him. The Newcastle striker had torn his anterior cruciate ligament and he would not return to action until April 2007. This injury led to protracted legal wrangling between Newcastle United and the FA over compensation payments, with the FA eventually having to pay out something in the region of £10 million, to cover Owen's wages, depreciation of his value, cost of a replacement striker and medical bills.

★ ★ ★

▦ HE'S A REBEL

▪ Fernando Redondo of Argentina refused to cut his hair, even though coach Daniel Passarella said he'd be axed from the squad after the 1994 World Cup if he didn't get a short back and sides. They couldn't come to an agreement, so Redondo was an absentee for Argentina in France in 1998, despite having just helped Real Madrid to Champions League success.

▪ Andrés Mazali, Olympic champion and all set to be Uruguay's star goalie at the first World Cup in 1930, was axed from the squad after breaking the coach's tough curfew rule.

▪ Antonio Rattin, the Argentine captain, refused to leave the field after being

sent off against England in the quarter-final in 1966.

■ The 1974 Russian team refused to play a qualifier play-off against Chile in a stadium where it was claimed political prisoners had been imprisoned and tortured. FIFA refused to listen, Chile kicked off against an empty half, scored into an empty net, and the match was duly abandoned!

The referee agreed – he should have worn a wig. The Argentinians were understandably furious.

■ Johan Cruyff chose not to take part with Holland in the 1978 finals, despite immense pressure and cash incentives offered by the Dutch FA. There were rumours it was on the grounds of Argentina's human rights record, while others blamed the 'Swimming Pool Incident' involving several players, young ladies and a hotel pool. But in 2008 he confirmed he was scared of leaving his family after a kidnapping attempt in 1977, where he and his wife Danny were tied up and threatened with guns in front of the Cruyff kids.

■ The 1986 Portuguese team went on strike over prize money, and refused to train between matches. They needn't have worried: they were straight on the plane home after the first round.

▦ VITAL PUB INFO
TO FOSTER FRIENDLY RELATIONS WITH FANS OF

CAMEROON

Fanspotter's guide

Green shirts, with dashes of rasta-ish red and yellow trim to match the Indomitable Lions' shorts and socks (and to help us distinguish them from fans of Nigeria).

Conversation starter

How come, in stamp albums, your country used to be called 'Cameroons'... just like Hartlepool United always used to be called 'Hartlepools'?

Accentuate the positive

Cameroon's first international football match was a 9-2 victory over French Somaliland in Madagascar, 1960.

Samuel Eto'o just couldn't ever impress the recycling fellas. Nobody ever knew why.

Skirt expertly around the negative

And they've never managed to improve on that result since, not in 50 years of trying.

Form guide

It was qualification at the last gasp, with new French coach Paul Le Guen picking up the pieces with four successive wins after an iffy start. A 2-0 away win over Morocco did the trick – but even so, they depended on Gabon upsetting Togo away from home. They were knocked out by Egypt in the quarter-finals of the African Cup of Nations.

One to watch

The 2010 World Cup represents Inter goalbanger Samuel Eto'o's best chance to shine on the World Cup stage. Cameroon didn't qualify for 2006 and were knocked out early in 2002, while back in 1998 Eto'o was the youngest player involved, aged just 17. Stepped up marvellously to his new role of skipper, scoring a world-beating nine in the qualifiers.

Simply the best... ever

Roger Milla – not because he was African Player of the Century, but because he somehow managed to be 38 in consecutive World Cup finals.

Useful French phrases

Samuel Eto'o: largement sur-evalue – Samuel Eto'o: vastly over-rated.

Soyez honnête. Avez-vous acheté un de ces kits sans manches? – Be honest. Did you ever buy one of those sleeveless kits?

Chat-up line

Here you go, love. A traditional gift of chicken gizzards for a guest who's so very welcome in this (public) house.

This one's on me

Palm wine, *s'il vous plait*.

Inside line on Cameroonian culture

It is considered disrespectful in Cameroon to cross your legs or wear a peaked hat in the presence of an older man, an official or a tribal elder. So, if you're dressed as an admiral and busting for a pee, it's probably best to re-arrange the meeting.

Common ground

There are four Cameroonians playing for English teams, with classy young Arsenal midfielder Alexandre Song the most likely headline-grabber. The rest are capable stoppers: there's André Bikey (Burnley), Sébastien Bassong and Benoît Assou-Ekotto (Spurs).

★ ★ ★

⠿ TALKING A GOOD GAME

Jesus Christ may be able to turn the other cheek but Luís Figo isn't Jesus Christ.

Portugal coach Luiz Felipe Scolari after Figo headbutted the Netherlands' Mark van Bommel in 2006

▦ ECCENTRIC BRIT BOSSES

Roy Hodgson

Croydon-born Fulham boss Hodgson was in charge of Switzerland at USA 1994, and also has the United Arab Emirates on his extremely weird CV, alongside Bristol City, Inter (twice), Blackburn and Neuchâtel Xamax. Not a lot of people know that he was in charge of Finland (the team, not the country) before taking up his present post at Fulham.

Andy Beattie

Scotland's boss Andy Beattie resigned after their very first match at the 1954 finals, having bickered with team officials after their defeat at the hands of fancied Austria. The next day, the Scots lost 7-0 to Uruguay. Point proven.

George Raynor

At the 1950 and 1958 finals, Sweden were managed by Yorkshireman Raynor, once a player with Aldershot and Bury. After the war, the Swedish national side crops up three times on George's CV, intermingled with names such as Åtvidaberg FF, Juventus, Lazio, Coventry City, Skegness Town, Djurgårdens IF and Doncaster Rovers. (And, yes, those clubs are in chronological order). Under Raynor, Sweden won the 1948 Olympic football title, came third at the 1950 World Cup, and were runners-up to Brazil in 1958.

Jack Butler

Ceylon-born Butler was a centre-half at Arsenal and Torquay between the end of the First World War and 1932, when he became a coach at the Belgian club Royal Daring. He took up the national team's reins for the 1938 World Cup finals before returning home to become trainer at Leicester City, then manager at Torquay, Crystal Palace and Colchester.

Jack Charlton

Northumberland-born Republic of Ireland boss Charlton was fined $14,000 and banned from the bench at USA 1994 for touchline scenes involving substitute John Aldridge and a famously useless fourth official, who took six minutes to OK Aldo's boots before he went on and grabbed a goal vital for progression to the next round. It was great fun listening to Jack and John giving the plodder a four-letter fusilade, all broadcast live – and even more delicious to discover via Jack's autobiography that he never paid the FIFA fine.

Bob Glendenning

He played in Barnsley's FA Cup-winning half-back line before the Great War, and for Accrington Stanley post-1918. But he really made his mark as the Dutch national coach for 15 years between 1925 and 1940. True, they bombed out of both the 1934 and 1938 World Cups in the first round, but Bob's still remembered in the Netherlands for his decent record of 36 wins in 87 games, and a formative Geordie version of Total Football.

★ ★ ★

▦ EBAY WORLD CUP
ON OFFER

£1,399.99 • 2002 World Cup ALL 64 Tickets MINT Condition STUNNING
'Unique Collection 25 MINT Used + 39 MINT COMPLETE/UNUSED.'
What a miserable, pointless waste...

£449.99 • Orig. Winner's Medal World Cup, Brazil 1950 – S.Conzalez
Aha, not an original medal but a commemorative jobbie dished out to the winning teams from 1924, 1928, 1930 and 1950 in 1975, to mark the 75th anniversary of the Association of Uruguayan Football Association.

£395! • FIFA World Cup As Seen On TV
The sell: 'A must for all football fans. As used by the press, media and television companies including the BBC.' The catch: A near-perfect resin replica, as proven by the fact that one of these was nicked from the Beeb amid a flurry of tabloid excitement during the 1998 World Cup. You'd have to be mad to want it – but then who could resist giving it a quick snog and holding it aloft over their head?

£249.99 • 1970 World Cup Finals Ticket – England v Czechoslovakia
Ah yes, the memories of this scintillating tie come, er, flooding back. A must for your mantelpiece, surely?

£4.99 • Scotland World Cup Memorabilia 1970s/80s
'You are bidding on a small selection of original Scotland World Cup souvenirs from 70s/80s, comprising: One "silk" scarf, about four foot long, fringed, with "Scotland for the Cup" on one side and "Scotland" the other. The material is quite thick, but definitely not silk. One "flat cap" the elasticated rim ensures one size fits all. One sew-on patch from Spain 1982. Although this stuff is 25+ years old it is in great nick as it's never been used, only stored!'

★ ★ ★

▦ THE UNOFFICIAL WORLD CHAMPIONSHIP

It's quite simple, gents: imagine football works in the same way as boxing. Every international match is a winner-takes-all affair and whoever beats the current 'World Champions' takes the title. Until they're defeated, that is, and the title is passed on to the team that beat them. And so on. We thought we'd begin with France's World Cup triumph in 1998 and see how the last decade or so could have unfolded had this method applied. However, the list actually begins on 30 November 1872, when England and Scotland met in the first-ever international (the match ended 0-0), and is correct to 2 March 2010.

Date	Venue	Comp	Teams	Result	New Holder	Held for (games)
12.07.1998	St. Denis	WC	France – Brazil	3–0	France	8
05.06.1999	St. Denis	ECQ	France – Russia	2–3	Russia	5
23.02.2000	Haifa	F	Israel – Russia	4–1	Israel	1
26.04.2000	Prague	F	Czech Rep – Israel	4–1	Czech Rep	0
03.06.2000	Nuremburg	F	Germany – Czech Rep	3–2	Germany	2
17.06.2000	Charleroi	EC	Germany – England	0–1	England	0
20.06.2000	Charleroi	EC	England – Romania	2–3	Romania	0
24.06.2000	Brussels	EC	Romania – Italy	0–2	Italy	1
02.07.2000	Rotterdam	EC	Italy – France	1–2	France	6
28.03.2001	Valencia	F	Spain – France	2–1	Spain	7
27.03.2002	Rotterdam	F	Netherlands – Spain	1–0	Netherlands	12
10.09.2003	Prague	ECQ	Czech Rep – Netherlands	3–1	Czech Rep	3
31.03.2004	Dublin	F	Ireland – Czech Rep	2–1	Ireland	2
29.05.2004	London	F	Ireland – Nigeria	0–3	Nigeria	2
20.06.2004	Luanda	WCQ	Angola – Nigeria	1–0	Angola	7
27.03.2005	Harare	WCQ	Zimbabwe – Angola	2–0	Zimbabwe	7
08.10.2005	Abuja	WCQ	Nigeria – Zimbabwe	5–1	Nigeria	0
16.11.2005	Bucharest	F	Romania – Nigeria	3–0	Romania	2
23.05.2006	Los Angeles	F	Romania – Uruguay	0–2	Uruguay	4
27.09.2006	Maracaibo	F	Venezuela – Uruguay	1–0	Venezuela	0
18.10.2006	Montevideo	F	Uruguay – Venezuela	4–0	Uruguay	0
15.11.2006	Tbilisi	F	Georgia – Uruguay	2–0	Georgia	1
24.03.2007	Glasgow	ECQ	Scotland – Georgia	2–1	Scotland	0
28.03.2007	Bari	ECQ	Italy – Scotland	2–0	Italy	2

Date	Venue	Comp	Teams	Result	New Holder	Held for (games)
22.08.2007	Budapest	F	Hungary – Italy	3–1	Hungary	1
12.09.2007	Istanbul	ECQ	Turkey – Hungary	3–0	Turkey	1
17.10.2007	Istanbul	ECQ	Turkey – Greece	0–1	Greece	5
24.05.2008	Budapest	F	Hungary – Greece	3–2	Hungary	3
10.09.2008	Solna	WCQ	Sweden – Hungary	2–1	Sweden	1
19.11.2008	Amsterdam	F	Netherlands – Sweden	3–1	Netherlands	12

WC World Cup   WCQ World Cup Qualifier   EC European Championships
ECQ European Championships Qualifier   F Friendly

Defence of the 'Title' (Top 5)

Since 1872, the 'unofficial' title has been held most by the following countries:

Team	Days Held	Last Held	Team	Days Held	Last Held
Scotland	13,003	28.03.2007	Argentina	2,443	04.07.1998
England	7,749	20.06.2000	Netherlands	2,167	02.03.2010
Ireland*	2,576	13.03.1920			

* NB. This refers to the united Ireland, before the creation of the Republic of Ireland and Northern Ireland.

Longest Defence of the 'Title' (Top 5)

- ▪ Scotland (20 games – 13.03.1880 to 17.03.1888)
- ▪ England (15 games – from 06.04.1891 to 04.04.1896)
- ▪ Germany (15 games – 30.06.1996 to 25.03.1998)
- ▪ Argentina (14 games – 18.06.1992 to 15.08.1993)
- ▪ Netherlands (14 games – 02.05.1973 to 07.07.1974)

Craig Beattie scores the goal that made Scotland 'unofficial' World Champions in March 2007.

This list is copyright © James Allnutt, Paul Crankshaw, Jostein Nygård, Roberto Di Maggio and RSSSF 2002/09. The full list can be found at http://rsssf.com/miscellaneous/unoff-wc.html. All rights reserved.

▦ VITAL PUB INFO
TO FOSTER FRIENDLY RELATIONS WITH FANS OF

ITALY

Fanspotter's guide

Sharp silk suits/blue football tops, button-down collars, Hush Puppies, hair gel, perfume – sitting in corner of snug bar where TV can be viewed, along with reflection of selves in cunning combination of mirrors.

Conversation starter

Not a lot of people know that Italy holds the Guinness World Record for being the country with the most lifts. (This fact, in combination with the slovenly pace of Serie A, suggests a nation that wholeheartedly embraces its laziness – a promising initial bond down the juicer).

Accentuate the positive

'The Italians cannot beat us,' quoth the cryptic Johan Cruyff, 'but we can certainly lose against them.' He said this before the Euro 2000 semi, but it's as true today as it ever was. Italy are the Cliff Thorburns – the 'grinders' – of world football.

Skirt expertly around the negative

French coach Gérard Houllier suggested in 2008 that the Italians were lucky to win the 2006 World Cup in Germany, specifically citing their second-round game against Australia – which, let's face it, was a steal.

Form guide

Unbeaten in qualifying with seven wins and three draws, they're the holders; they've got an easy group, facing Slovakia, New Zealand and Paraguay. But Fabio Capello has put a kibosh on the Azzurri's chances by getting just a little ahead of the game: 'I would love a final between England and Italy. For Italy, for me and for all of us. The strangest moment will be during the national anthems. But, I am wearing a different shirt now and I must work for the England shirt.'

One to watch

Italy are suddenly looking a bit creaky (as in 'old') at the back, with Buffon (31) in goal, and a back four potentially including Fabio Cannavaro (36), Gianluca Zambrotta (32) and Nicola Legrottaglie (33). Then there's Milan's Andrea Pirlo (30) and Gennaro Gattuso (31) in midfield with Juve's Mauro Camoranesi (33). With just one World Cup under his belt, Fiorentina's Alberto Gilardino (27) is almost the baby of the team, but he's the form striker.

Simply the best... ever

Zoff? Zola? Del Piero? Riva? Gianni Rivera played 501 Serie A games for Milan's Rossoneri between 1960 and 1979, scoring 160 goals. The Golden Boy was a hero in Italy's romp through the 1970 World Cup, where he was deployed as a devastatingly effective supersub; inexplicably, however, he made no appearance in their final thrashing against Brazil. History might have been different had coach Ferruccio Valcareggi not insisted that Rivera and Sandro Mazzola 'couldn't play together'.

Useful Italian phrases

Mi scusi signore. Questa è la mia fidanzata. Si prega di interrompere l'occhiolino al suo – Excuse me, sir – that's my girlfriend. Please stop winking at her.

Mi scusi, signore. Questa è la mia nonna. Si prega di interrompere l'occhiolino al suo – Excuse me, sir – that's my grandmother. Please stop winking at her.

Non sono sicuro di quello che mia nonna sta facendo neppure qui. Sono confusa quanto si – I am not sure what my grandmother is doing here either. I am as confused as you are.

Chat-up line

Let me be your *fantasista* (Italian for playmaker – beware if she puts up a *catenaccio* defence).

This one's on me

Espresso, grappa or red, red wine. But never all three at once.

Inside line on Italian culture

'The English say "Yours Truly" and mean it. The Italians say "I kiss your feet" and they mean "I kick your head".' (Wilfred Owen)

Common ground

Traditionally, an Italian priest visiting the dying would rest his hat at the end of the bed. It is still considered bad luck to rest your hat at the end of someone's bed. Beware the words *cappello sul letto* (hat on the bed). Interesting side note: it is also considered unlucky to rest Fabio Capello on the end of a dying person's bed.

★ ★ ★

⠿ WORLD CUP SONGS
USA 1994

Die Fußballnationalmannschaft & Village People • 'Far Away In America'
(Number 1 in Germany)
The sheer depression of England failing to make the cut was leavened ever
so slightly by the prospect of the German World Cup Squad joining up
with the Village People to sing their official anthem. Did they think it was
cool to dress up as New York cops and leather disco victims and gyrate
atop construction sites? Did they know something we didn't? Maybe the
band hadn't sunk without trace in Germany, but had been enjoying a steady
string of European hits these past 15 years? Or, the most delicious prospect,
did we know something they didn't? After all, it happened before in 1979,
when the US Navy had considered using 'In The Navy' in a recruitment ad,
only cancelling the campaign once the guys had strutted their stuff all over
the poop deck of a warship...

The frisson of *schadenfreude* was redoubled by the USA's official single –
ahem, 'Gloryland' by Daryl Hall and the Sounds Of Blackness. It was all
easily enough to eclipse the pleasures offered by our
own representatives, The Republic of Ireland World
Cup Squad, with the weird Neighbourhood Watch
singalong 'Watch Your House For Ireland'.

There was no clear
winner in the Gary
Neville lookalike
competition.

▥ WHAT THE PAPERS SAY

The *Independent*'s coverage of Italia 90 brought out some familiar themes: 'A wretched sense of déjà vu enveloped Scotland and their followers in Genoa yesterday as Costa Rica, supposedly the weakest team in Group C if not the entire tournament, joined Peru and Iran among their catalogue of World Cup calamities.'

If it wasn't one thing, it was another, as the report on the Argentina v Soviet Union match showed: 'Maradona blocked Kusnetsov's near-post header with his arm. A penalty? Apparently not, when the culprit is in partnership with The Almighty.' Speaking of penalties, Patrick Barclay knew what was to come when England were forced into a penalty shoot-out against West Germany: 'England survived their third successive ordeal by extra-time last night in Turin, but far, far worse was to come: defeat in a penalty contest, the same fate as Italy had endured 24 hours earlier.'

However, there were some new stories, not least the emergence of the African nations as a genuine threat in the tournament, with one man showing the way during the Cameroon v Colombia match, as Norman Fox reported: 'Roger Milla is fast becoming the unlikely star of this World Cup. He came out of semi-retirement to be here and showed yesterday how to be decisive when all around him seem afraid to take positive action.' The growing financial muscle of football was also clear in John Moynihan's report: 'H.G.Wells would have been delighted by the giant flying saucer shape of San Nicola as seen from the new winding motorway, which has crushed through pretty vineyards and olive groves all for the sake of World Cup footie.'

As so often, some of the best stories came from the Irish camp, as reported by Joe Lovejoy at their game against Italy: 'With half time approaching the scufflers were holding their own comfortably enough for Charlton's salmon pink face to crease into a broad smile for the television cameras – before he told the cameramen to "bugger off".'

But in the end, it came down to a penalty and a very familiar outcome when the taker was a German: 'The last penalty of the World Cup gave the trophy to West Germany here last night. Seven minutes from the end of a match they had dominated throughout Andreas Brehme stroked the ball wide of Sergio Goycochea.'

★ ★ ★

⣿ THE YASHIN AWARD

Since 1994 this award, named after the USSR's legendary goalkeeper Lev Yashin, is awarded to the best goalkeeper of the tournament according to the FIFA Technical Study Group. Prior to 1994 the best goalkeeper was considered to be the one named in the All-Star Team. Despite playing in the 1958, 1962 and 1966 World Cups, Yashin never made the All-Star Team:

- 1930 Uruguay — Enrique Ballesteros — Uruguay
- 1934 Italy — Ricardo Zamora — Spain
- 1938 France — Frantisek Plánicka — Czechoslovakia
- 1950 Brazil — Roque Máspoli — Uruguay
- 1954 Switzerland — Gyula Grosics — Hungary
- 1958 Sweden — Harry Gregg — Northern Ireland
- 1962 Chile — Viliam Schrojf — Czechoslovakia
- 1966 England — Gordon Banks — England
- 1970 Mexico — Ladislao Mazurkiewicz — Uruguay
- 1974 West Germany — Jan Tomaszewski — Poland
- 1978 Argentina — Ubaldo Fillol — Argentina
- 1982 Spain — Dino Zoff — Italy
- 1986 Mexico — Harald Schumacher — West Germany
- 1990 Italy — Sergio Goycochea — Argentina
- 1994 USA — Michel Preud'homme — Belgium
- 1998 France — Fabien Barthez — France
- 2002 Korea/Japan — Oliver Kahn — Germany
- 2006 Germany — Gianluigi Buffon — Italy

And there is 'The Clown', Polish goalkeeper Jan Tomaszewski, stopping England going to the 1974 World Cup finals. Thanks for that one Cloughie.

⠿ VITAL PUB INFO
TO FOSTER FRIENDLY RELATIONS WITH FANS OF

PARAGUAY

Fanspotter's guide
Look out for red and white stripes, coupled not with a Southampton burr, a Stokey twang or a Mackem howay, but a spee-dy-Span-eeesh-mo-no-tone (and blue shorts).

Conversation starter
'Paraguay is nowhere and famous for nothing,' according to satirist P.J. O'Rourke. But just who is Roque Santa Cruz? Exactly. No idea.

Accentuate the positive
Fourth in the 2001 Under-20 World Cup and runners-up in the 2004 Olympics suggests a squad about to reach maturity.

Skirt expertly around the negative
Realistically, they are 66-1 outsiders.

Form guide
Finished third in South American qualifying – just one point behind top-placed Brazil. They beat Brazil, Argentina and Chile along the way, and more recently drew 0-0 in an away friendly with the Netherlands.

One to watch
Salvador Cabanas, prolific striker currently with Club América in Mexico.

Simply the best... ever
José Luis Chilavert, goalkeeper/goalscorer extraordinaire. He not only picked up the IFFHS World's Best Goalie award three times, but scored a record 62 times in his career from thunderous free kicks and penalties.

Useful Spanish phrases
Les dimos una paliza en Alemania 2006. ¿Te acuerdas? – We gave you a whipping at Germany 2006. Remember that?

Es el nombre de 'Uruguay' divertido para ti también? – Is the name 'Uruguay' funny to you also?

Salvador Cabanas attacks the Colombian defence, but will he finally become someone famous for Paraguayans to boast about (apart from Roque Santa Cruz, of course)?

Eso es Mark Lawrenson. Él es un bufón. – That is Mark Lawrenson. He is a buffoon. (Useful when watching televised games in the pub.)

Chat-up line

Your beautiful country is known as *Corazón de América* – the Heart of America – and surely it was named after you.

This one's on me

Mate (pronounced 'Mah-Tay') – a type of tea made from the leaves of a species of holly native to sub-tropical South America. *Mate* is a huge part of daily life in Paraguay (as well as in Argentina and Uruguay) – you'll even see people riding motorbikes with beakers of the stuff under their arms.

Inside line on Paraguayan culture

'I terrified myself the other day by trying to write a list of all the things in this world we don't need. All the things that, if they didn't exist, no one would miss them... The countries Chad, Paraguay and Laos. Unnecessary.' (Armando Iannucci, 2001)

Common ground

Unmarried President Fernando Lugo, elected in 2008, named his sister, Mercedez Lugo, as the country's first lady. Rumours that the Lugo family have their roots in Norfolk are still unconfirmed.

★ ★ ★

▦ TALKING A GOOD GAME

Nigerian culture minister Otumba Runshewe wasn't keen on Taribo West's hairstyle in France 1998.

> Our youths copy our footballers, but the players seem to forget that braids embrace a sense of homosexuality in the developing world. We certainly don't want that.

ONE-PLAYER COUNTRIES

They're the only player – possibly even the only person – that anyone from anywhere else in the world could name from that country:

- Liberia – George Weah
- Trinidad & Tobago – Dwight Yorke
- Costa Rica – Paolo Wanchope
- Mali – Freddie Kanoute
- Guinea – Titi Camara
- South Korea – Park Ji-Sung
- Montserrat – Ruel Fox
- Zanzibar – Freddie Mercury
- Paraguay – José Luis Chilavert
- Estonia – Mart Poom
- Togo – Emmanuel Adebayor
- Peru – Teofilo Cubillas (oh, and Nobby Solano)
- Bermuda – Shaun Goater (oh yeah – and Clyde Best!)
- Nicaragua – Bianca Jagger

★ ★ ★

WHATEVER HAPPENED TO THE HEROES?

Ray Houghton • Ireland 1990, 1994

Cosmopolitan Ray was born in Glasgow, played in England, and turned out 73 times for Ireland, for whom he qualified through his dad. Ireland went out to the Italians in the 1990 quarter-finals, but got their revenge four years later courtesy of Ray's early goal, a dipping 25-yard shot followed by that iconic forward roll. Not a lot of people know that his pro debut came at West Ham – his sole appearance as a sub – followed by a steady rise at Fulham and Oxford, before his big move to Liverpool. Ray was a terrier-like Red between 1987 and 1992 before heading on to Aston Villa, Crystal Palace, Reading and Stevenage Borough. He's now a pundit, with talkSPORT and RTÉ high on his CV.

Salvatore 'Totò' Schillaci • Italy 1990

The 1990 World Cup is still remembered today by Italian football fans as the *Notti Magiche di Totò Schillaci* (magical nights of Totò Schillaci), even though the team came only third in their home tournament. He won the Golden

'You cannot be serious!' Oh, but we are. You've come from nowhere to make yourself famous. That's what the World Cup is all about, you goggle-eyed loon.

Boot with six goals, and his bulging eyes and beseeching, pleading (for dodgy penalties) face sticks in the mind as a symbol of the event. It was enough to get him star role in an Irish TV ad for Smithwick's beer, based on his scoring to eliminate Ireland from 1990 and their sweet revenge in USA 94. Today he lives in his native Palermo, where he runs a kids' football academy.

Ernest Wilimowski • Poland 1938
Ernest went down in history as the first player ever to score four goals in a World Cup finals match, going on the rampage for Poland against Brazil in 1938 – and yet still finished up on the losing side, 6-5. However, Ernest scored 21 goals in 22 games for his country before succumbing to Nazi pressure and switching to German nationality (Ernest had been born Otto Pradella to German parents, later taking his stepfather's name). Reviled as a traitor in Poland after the war, and written out of history for long decades, he was later asked why he agreed to represent the Third Reich, which had overrun his country. Having saved his mother from Auschwitz, where she was interned for dating a Polish Jew, he admitted honestly, 'Because I was scared.'

★ ★ ★

▦ OLDIES BUT GOLDIES XI

These old boys weigh in at an impressive combined age of 414. Stretched end to end they would reach from the 2010 World Cup back to 1596, when England were still celebrating their recent triumph against the odds over Spain.

1 Dino Zoff, 40 • Italy The legendary Italian net-minder gets the nod just ahead of England's Peter Shilton. Although both were 40 years old when they played their last World Cup match, Zoff actually got to lift the trophy in Spain in 1982.

2 Fernando Clavijo, 37 • USA You can take the man out of Uruguay but you can't take Uruguay out of the man. Clavijo became the oldest player to be sent off in the World Cup when he was shown the red card with five minutes remaining of the USA's second round game against Brazil on 4 July 1994. What a way to celebrate Independence Day.

3 Jan Heintze, 38 • Denmark When Peter Schmeichel retired in 2001, left-back Jan Heintze was given the captain's armband for the 2002 tournament. However, at the age of 38, Heintze struggled with the heat in Korea and was substituted in the first game against Uruguay. The captaincy was handed on to Rene Henriksen for the last group game, against France, and Heintze also watched the 3-0 defeat to England in Niigata from the bench.

4 Lothar Matthäus, 37 • Germany The German midfielder holds the record for number of tournaments played as an outfield player (five – 1982, 1986, 1990, 1994 and 1998), and also the most World Cup matches played – 25. He played his last World Cup game aged 37, and clocked up 150 caps for West Germany/Germany. As Lothar himself said: 'I am an idol in Germany and I should be treated like one.'

5 Giuseppe Bergomi, 34 • Italy After being dismissed against Norway in a Euro 1992 qualifier, Bergomi's international career appeared to be over. But he was recalled to the national side by Cesare Maldini for the 1998 World Cup. He played against Austria and Norway, before making his last World Cup appearance in the quarter-final defeat against France.

6 Björn Nordqvist, 35 • Sweden The big blond centre-half was 35 by the time he went to Argentina in 1978 for his third World Cup finals tournament. After that, he left IFK Göteborg and was put out to pasture at Minnesota Kicks.

7 Stanley Matthews, 39 • England The Wizard of the Dribble, Stanley Matthews was 39 years old when he appeared in England's final match of the 1954 World Cup, a quarter-final against Uruguay. He was hardly past his sell-by date, however, continuing to play professional football in the top division until the age of 50.

8 Roger Milla, 42 • Cameroon Milla signed for his first club, Douala, at the age of 13 in 1965. Just 25 years later he achieved global fame, scoring four times for Cameroon at the 1990 World Cup. His goals against Romania and Colombia helped the Indomitable Lions to the quarter-finals and his celebratory corner flag dance helped make him an unforgettable figure. In 1994 Milla scored against Russia in a 6-1 defeat, though he had the consolation of a place in the record books as the oldest scorer of a World Cup goal.

9 Tom Finney, 36 • England Preston North End's renowned winger played in the 1950, 1954 and 1958 World Cup tournaments. When he slotted home a late penalty against the Soviet Union in Gothenburg to earn England a 2-2 draw, he became the oldest England player to score in a World Cup, a record that still stands.

'Sorry, love. I think I've left me monkey wrench in the back of the net.'

10 Ángel Labruna, 39 • Argentina A legendary striker for River Plate and Argentina, Labruna was robbed of the opportunity to play in the World Cup until the twilight of his career; firstly by the Second World War, and then by Argentina's decision not to compete in 1950 and 1954. Labruna was 39 when he played his first World Cup game, against Northern Ireland in 1958. His second, and last, game saw a 6-1 thrashing by Czechoslovakia.

11 Nílton Santos, 37 • Brazil Santos, a left-sided wing-back, was a non-playing squad member in 1950 when Brazil hosted the tournament, but he became a regular in sides of 1954, 1958 and 1962. He was 37 years old when he won his second World Cup winner's medal in Chile in 1962.

▦ VITAL PUB INFO
TO FOSTER FRIENDLY RELATIONS WITH FANS OF

NEW ZEALAND

Fanspotter's guide
Listen out for curiously polite-sounding Antipodeans dancing a Maori *haka*. They'll be wearing white shirts – perhaps unsurprisingly, given that their team is nicknamed the 'All Whites'.

Conversation starter
Rugby is rubbish, isn't it?

Accentuate the positive
They made the finals in 1982, and memorably gave mighty Scotland a scare when they scored twice to pull them back to 3-2.

Skirt expertly around the negative
They lost 5-2 in the end. And, to be honest, they're present in South Africa only because Australia opted to jump out of the Oceania qualifying group and into Asia-Pacific.

Form guide
Beating tiny Pacific coral outcrops is akin to taking candy off an Under-15s park team. They did get past Bahrain (fifth best in Asia) to qualify via the play-offs, but could easily find themselves outclassed even against relative minnows.

Four to watch
Blackburn midfielder Ryan Nelsen commands most respect; other Brit Kiwis include Celtic striker Chris Killen and Plymouth's Rory Fallon, while West Brom attacker Chris Wood is one for the future.

Simply the best... ever
Billy Walsh played 350 games for Manchester City between 1936 and 1951, as well as representing four national sides: England Schoolboys, the Republic of Ireland, Northern Ireland and New Zealand. Having retired Down Under, he came out of retirement aged 40 to skipper the national side to victory in grudge match against an English FA XI.

Useful Maori phrases
Kia ora – Hello.
Ka Pirangi koe ki te kanikani tahi taua? – Would you like to dance with me?

Chat-up line
Grouse, you're a beaut dag. I'm so stoked you've turned my world to custard.

This one's on me
There's a Kiwi ad for Tui beer that has spawned the catchphrase 'Yeah, right'. That's as in 'All-Whites for the World Cup? Yeah, right.'
Inside line on Kiwi culture
Their wildest rock band ever? It's those devil-may-care axemen, Crowded House.
Common ground
Queenie is the Kiwis' head of state, and it's New Zealand lamb for dinner this Sunday. In truth, the Yanks will be rooting for the Kiwis more than the Brits, as Stanford old-boy Nelsen and three other regulars attended soccer college in the States.

★ ★ ★

▦ TOP TEN SHOCKS

1 England v USA, 1950
After remaining aloof from the first three World Cups, England finally joined FIFA and deigned to join the party after the Second World War. Very soon they would be wondering about the wisdom of that decision, playing Goliath to the United States' David. The 1950 World Cup, held in Brazil, started according to the script for England, with a 2-0 win over Chile in the Maracana, thanks to goals from Stan Mortensen and Wilf Mannion.

But on 29 June in the Estadio Independencia, Belo Horizonte, England suffered utter humiliation at the hands of a group of amateurs loosely affiliated to the USA. A strong England side that included Wilf Mannion, Tom Finney, Alf Ramsey, Stan Mortensen and Billy Wright (Stanley Matthews was rested) lost to a 38th minute goal scored by Haitian Joe Gaetjens, who waited on tables for a living. England hit the woodwork four times, one effort was 'cleared' from a yard behind the goal line; England keeper Bert Williams did not touch the ball in the second half; and Mortensen was rugby tackled by Charlie Colombo when clear on goal... but an equaliser never came. Back home, some newspapers assumed the scoreline to be a typing error and credited England with a 10-1 victory.

2 Argentina v Cameroon, 1990
Italia 90's curtain-raiser at the Stadio Giuseppe Meazza, Milan, paired defending champions Argentina with Cameroon, and nobody gave the

Francois Omam-Biyik scores Cameroon's winner against the reigning World Champions.

Africans a hope in hell; but the 'Indomitable Lions' were no wide-eyed innocents, having returned home from Spain 82 unbeaten, drawing with Italy, Poland and Peru.

They beat eventual finalists Argentina with a subtle blend of skill and extreme violence. After soaking up pressure from the Argentinians for the first hour of the game, Cameroon had André Kana-Biyik dismissed. Incredibly, the ten men then took the lead when François Omam-Biyik rose athletically to plant a downward header that squirmed under keeper Nery Pumpido and over the line.

Cameroon were further reduced when Benjamin Massing was sent off for an almost poetically savage foul on Claudio Caniggia. Caniggia picked up a loose ball in his own half and sprinted up the park, twice he had his heels clipped, and ran his last 20 yards with his body way ahead of his legs, desperately trying to regain his balance, before Massing moved in with a *coup de grâce* that left the blond striker poleaxed and lying still on the turf. Nine-man Cameroon held out for the remaining few minutes before the final whistle heralded wild scenes of celebration.

3 Scotland v Peru, 1978

Scotland began their Argentinian adventure in Cordoba, riding on a huge wave of Ally McLeod-inspired overconfidence. They got off to a decent start when Peru keeper Ramón Quiroga spilled a shot from Bruce Rioch, allowing Joe Jordan to open the scoring in the 14th minute; but three minutes before

'Oh great, you get a scratchy nylon shirt worth nothing and I get a J-cloth. At least you'll be back before the postcards again.'

the break, Peru unzipped Scotland's defence and César Cueto fired an equaliser past Alan Rough.

On the hour the Scots wasted a chance to re-establish their lead after Rioch had been scythed down in the area by Hector Chumpitaz. Don Masson's poor spot kick was easily blocked by Quiroga and Scotland's spirits seemed to slump. Teofilo Cubillas gave Peru a 72nd-minute advantage with a superb free kick struck with the outside of his foot. Five minutes later Cubillas found the top left-hand corner of Rough's goal again, this time with a shot on the run from 25 yards.

In some ways, this wasn't one of the World Cup's biggest upsets: Peru were a decent side who won the group which also included the Netherlands, and Scotland had never progressed past the first round. But Ally McLeod had created an illusion that Scotland were invincible, thanks to a squad boasting such stars as Buchan, Rioch, Dalglish, Jordan and Souness. In one evening their high hopes had been brought to earth with a bump.

4 Spain v Northern Ireland, 1982

Billy Bingham played at outside-right for Northern Ireland in all five of their games in the 1958 World Cup in Sweden; the next time they qualified, in 1982, Bingham was the manager. Northern Ireland drew 0-0 with Yugoslavia and 1-1 with Honduras, before facing Spain in the final group game, knowing that a win would ensure they qualified.

After a bruising first-half, the Irish stunned the 50,000 crowd in the Estadio Luis Casanova, Valencia, when they took the lead two minutes after the break. Gerry Armstrong went on a surging run and fed Billy Hamilton down the right. His cross was intercepted by Arconada who only succeeded in teeing up Armstrong with a chance which he smashed home from ten yards.

Northern Ireland had 43 minutes to hang on, which looked even less likely when Mal Donaghy was sent off with half an hour remaining. But a combination of luck, gritty determination, and veteran keeper Pat Jennings in great form, saw Northern Ireland hold out for a famous victory, topping Group 5. Billy Bingham beamed from ear to ear as he hugged his captain Martin O'Neill – having emulated his own achievement as a player in making it into Round Two.

5 Costa Rica v Scotland, 1990

Drawn in Group C alongside Brazil and Sweden, Scotland's best hope of a win appeared to be in their opening game at the Stadio Luigi Ferraris, Genoa, against World Cup debutants Costa Rica. But well-travelled coach Bora Milutinović had the Costa Ricans moulded into a tight unit capable of a decent passing game. After Scotland had pushed forward throughout the first half to no avail, the underdogs took the lead four minutes into the second half. A sweeping move upfield saw seven passes pinged around, then a smart back-heel executed by Claudio Jara allowed Juan Cayasso the time and space to slot the ball past Jim Leighton.

Scotland had 40 minutes to retrieve the situation, but they found goalkeeper Gabelo Conejo in excellent form. His finest moment saw him block a Mo Johnston effort from point-blank range. Scotland could not find a way through and the final whistle saw their hopes of progressing into the knockout stages in tatters. Although the Scots beat Sweden 2-1, so did Costa Rica, and they proudly took second place in Group C, behind Brazil.

6 North Korea v Italy, 1966

North Korea qualified for their first World Cup in 1966 but were unsure what sort of reception they would get from the people of Middlesbrough, just 13 years after the end of the Korean War. They needn't have worried; Teesside's football fans welcomed them with open arms and cheered them to the rafters in their three games at Ayresome Park. After a 3-0 defeat against the USSR and a 1-1 draw with Chile, it looked as though the Koreans would be bowing out after their last Group 4 game against Italy.

But a Pak Doo Ik strike in the 42nd minute was the only goal of the game and a stunned Italy returned home to the traditional rotten tomatoes reception. The Koreans almost pulled off an even bigger shock in their quarter-final at Goodison Park, going 3-0 up against Portugal within 25 minutes. But Eusebio then scored four times, Portugal won 5-3, and normal service was resumed.

7 South Korea v Italy, 2002

Having lost to North Korea in 1966, Italy completed the set in 2002, suffering defeat at the hands of co-hosts South Korea in a second-

'How many times do we have to tell you about the [legally verifiable] Italian tradition of match-fixing?'

round tie in Daejeon. You would be hard pressed to find an Italian who accepts the scoreline at face value, however, with conspiracy theories claiming that South Korea were being 'helped' towards the final.

In the fourth minute, Christian Panucci hauled Seol Ki-Hyeon to the ground in the area, but Ahn Jung-Hwan's spot kick was brilliantly saved by Gianluigi Buffon. The Azzurri then went ahead in the 18th minute when Christian Vieri nodded home from a corner. Italy decided to sit on their lead and clammed up, a tactic that almost worked until the 88th minute when a defensive error from Panucci allowed Seol Ki-Hyeon in for an equaliser.

Extra time saw Ecuadorian referee Byron Moreno mired in controversy. He showed Francesco Totti a yellow card for diving in the penalty area when he had clearly had his trailing leg kicked and had a poke in the eye for good measure. It was his second caution, so Mr Moreno solemnly raised the red card. Ten-man Italy then scored what proved to be a legitimate goal, but Damiano Tommasi was incorrectly flagged offside. With three minutes of extra time remaining, Ahn Jung-Hwan made amends for his penalty miss, heading home the Golden Goal winner and heightening Italy's seething sense of injustice. They had already had four 'goals' disallowed in the tournament, and were convinced that they had been nobbled. The quarter-final match between Spain and South Korea did nothing to allay the Italians' suspicions, with Ruben Baraja and Fernando Morientes both having seemingly good goals ruled out before the Koreans progressed to the semi-finals.

8 Senegal v France, 2002

Senegal, playing in their first World Cup, sensationally beat their former colonial masters, World Cup holders and European Champions France in the opening game of the 2002 tournament. Les Bleus, who were missing an injured Zinédine Zidane, looked a shadow of the side that had beaten Brazil in the final four years earlier.

After half an hour, El Hadji Diouf charged down the left before squaring the ball for Bouba Diop, who took advantage of ponderous defending to net from close in. He ran to the corner flag, took off his shirt, laid it carefully on the turf and, joined by his team-mates, did a funny little dance round it. Although Thierry Henry struck the crossbar with a shot from the edge of the area, the scoreline remained 1-0 and Senegal ended the game as worthy winners. They progressed into the second round where they beat Sweden 2-1, before losing 1-0 to Turkey in the quarter-finals. France drew 0-0 with Uruguay, lost 2-0 to Denmark and went home with out scoring a goal. They were the first reigning World Cup champions since Brazil in 1966 to be eliminated at the group stage.

9 Algeria v West Germany, 1982

When European Champions West Germany faced Algeria (in their first World Cup) in Gijon, no one gave the Desert Foxes a chance, certainly not German coach Jupp Derwall who promised: 'If we don't beat Algeria I'll take the next train home!'

But Algeria, playing an exciting brand of attacking football, took the lead early in the second half when Rabah Madjer seized on a loose ball after a Harald Schumacher save. That improbable lead lasted just 13 minutes before Karl-Heinz Rummenigge restored parity, sliding into the six-yard box to meet a low cross from the left. But the North Africans' spirits were not dampened, and straight from the kick-off they poured forward, Lakhdar Belloumi producing a carbon copy of Rummenigge's goal to regain the lead. This time, despite several close calls, there was no way back for Germany and the final whistle sparked wild celebrations from Algeria's players and supporters. Sadly Algeria did not reap the reward for their great achievement, West Germany and Austria conspiring to claim first and second slots in Group 2 for themselves... and Jupp Derwall never did catch that train.

10 Italy v Ireland, 1994

Italy met the Republic of Ireland in the Giants Stadium, East Rutherford, New Jersey in the opening game of Group E. The Irish and Italians from New York arrived *en masse* and there were over 75,000 fans who witnessed

Ireland's giant-killing act. The kick-off was delayed when both teams lined up in the tunnel wearing white shirts, but after the Irish had changed into their traditional green, they didn't have to wait long for something to celebrate. From 25 yards Ray Houghton floated a majestic shot over Italian keeper Gianluca Pagliuca and under the crossbar, sending the Irish contingent wild with delight.

A five-man midfield and an inspired performance by centre-half Paul McGrath kept the Italians at bay for the remaining 79 minutes of the game, before the supporters set off to paint New Jersey and New York green. Ireland lost to Mexico and drew with Norway and for the first and to date only time a World Cup group ended with all four teams level on four points. Ireland and Italy could not be separated by goal difference or goals scored, so Ireland progressed because they had beaten Italy when the teams played each other. Italy also sneaked through as one of the best third-placed teams and made it all the way to the final, while Ireland lost 2-0 to the Netherlands in the second round.

★ ★ ★

▦ TALKING A GOOD GAME

Brazil's Luiz Mendes on the 1962 World Cup, quoted in *World Cup Stories,* Chris Hunt (2006)

The manager went to see Garrincha and said: 'Look, Pelé is not able to play. You have to play good enough for you and Pelé too.' Garrincha said: 'Yeah, okay, leave it with me no problem.'

⠿ ENGLISH REFS' BIG DECISIONS

■ Jack Taylor had to hold up the kick-off of the 1974 World Cup final because all the corner and halfway flags had gone missing.

■ He then gave a penalty to the Netherlands in the first minute, before West Germany had even touched the ball.

■ In the filth-fest that was the so-called 'Battle of Berne' in 1954, Brazilian Humberto Tozzi begged ref Arthur Ellis on his knees not to send him off – but was still sent packing, in tears.

■ Clive Thomas whistled for time a split second before a Zico 'goal' flew into the net, for Brazil against Sweden in the 1978 finals.

■ In 2006, Graham Poll booked Croatian Josip Šimunić three times in one match – in the 61st, 90th and 93rd minutes.

Poll makes a terrible mistake – he books the wrong player for sitting down.

★ ★ ★

VITAL PUB INFO
TO FOSTER FRIENDLY RELATIONS WITH FANS OF

SLOVAKIA

Fanspotter's guide
The Slovakian rough-haired pointer is a dog, not a big-screen fan.

Conversation starter
Did you know pop artist Andy Warhol was of Slovakian descent?

Accentuate the positive
When do you reckon Slovakia played their first international as an independent nation? 1994? Wrong. It was against Germany in 1939. And they won 2-0!

Skirt expertly around the negative

Sadly, this seems to have angered the Germans, who promptly invaded.

Form guide

Beat Poland, Northern Ireland and Slovenia to qualify, plus the USA in a post-qualification friendly, but lost to Chile. England beat Slovakia 4-0 in a Wembley friendly in March 2009, so we're not too bovvered.

One to watch

Ten goals in 29 starts for Slovakia make Stanislav Šesták the striker most likely to. He plays for VfL Bochum in the Bundesliga.

Simply the best... ever

Marek Mintál's goalscoring prowess in the Slovakian league translated into similar form for Nuremberg of the Bundesliga, where he's now starred for seven seasons.

Useful Slovak phrases

Mozeme poprosit capovane pivo, flaskove pivo – A draught lager and a bottle of lager, please. (Useful because Slovaks like lager.)

Znamenas pre mna vsetko – You mean everything to me. (Yes, even as much as lager.)

Chat-up line

As Slovaks can seem reserved and formal, rarely referring to strangers by first names, perhaps we could break the ice at one of the country's 1,100 hot mudbaths.

This one's on me

Bryndzové halušky is a national dish consisting of boiled lumps of potato dumpling with bryndza sheep cheese and bacon. Best washed down with lager.

Inside line on Slovak culture

Tennis champ Martina Hingis is the most famous Slovakian. Your new friends most likely went to school with her and will be able tell you some proper stories.

Common ground

The Slovak capital Bratislava straddles the Blue Danube. It's the new Prague – a popular spot for stag dos and other lager-related trips.

★ ★ ★

▦ THE GREAT WORLD CUP MYSTERY

When Brazil won the Jules Rimet trophy for the third time in 1970, FIFA presented it to them permanently and commissioned a new 'World Cup' for the 1974 tournament in West Germany. Silvio Gazzaniga, a sculptor from Milan, headed a field of 53 designs. Gazzaniga said of the figures supporting the globe: 'He had to be a hero, but a hero with the qualities of someone who has worked hard and suffered, who his fellow humans will identify with.' When this new trophy was first presented to 1974 winners West Germany it had a yellow, glowing matt finish; but over the years it seems to have been polished to a more shiny, reflective finish.

In 2006 it had to be repaired, soon after the Italians had been presented with it, because a piece of the green malachite that circles the base had broken off. Italian newspaper *Il Messaggero* showed photos taken through the window of the coach that took the team from Pratica di Mare airbase to Rome for the official homecoming celebrations. A concerned-looking Fabio Cannavaro is holding a jelly baby-sized green piece, while several team-mates look on in dismay. The paper insinuated that the Italians' celebrations had got out of hand, with players witnessed kissing the trophy, licking it, shouting at it and putting a hat on it. No one has ever offered an explanation as to why it ended up broken and the day was saved with a dab of glue.

★ ★ ★

▦ WORLD CUP HEADLINES

YOU'LL NEVER WALK COLOGNE
The *Sun* ahead of England's final Group B game against Sweden, 2006
ZZ STOP AFTER WORLD CUP
Sporting Life on Zinédine Zidane's announcement of his retirement after the 2006 World Cup
OUTCHA! – ARGIES GET THEIR OWN BACK ON US
The *Sun* after Maradona's 'Hand of God' goal in 1986
THREE LIONS IN AFRICA
Daily Mirror on England qualifying for South Africa 2010
10 HEROIC LIONS... ONE STUPID BOY
Becks gets it in the neck from the *Daily Mirror* after his sending off against Argentina in 1998

BECKHAM PUTS THE WORLD TO RIGHTS
The Times on England's 1-0 revenge over Argentina, 2002
THESE ARE THE WORLD CHAMPIONS
The early edition of *O Mundo* in Rio jumps the gun, printing this above
a picture of the Brazilian players in 1950. They lost 2-1 to Uruguay.

★ ★ ★

▦ SELECTION HEADACHES

■ In the 1930 finals, Romania's newly crowned King Carol II not only
ordered his national side to take part, safeguarding their jobs while giving
them three months off work – he then went ahead and selected the team!
They beat Peru 3-1, but crashed 4-0 to the Uruguayan hosts.

■ In 1938, Brazil boss Ademar Pimenta rested Leonidas for the semi against
Italy. 'The Black Diamond', the tournament's eventual
top scorer with seven goals, hit the back of the net in
every round he played, but Brazil lost 2-1 and had to
console themselves with victory in the third-place play-
off when Leonidas scored twice.

It was men against boys for Leonidas. Huge Swedish men against particularly slight young Brazilian boys.

■ Scotland's first-ever World Cup showing at the 1954 finals was crippled by Rangers electing to hold back their players to go on a pre-season tour of friendlies. Scotland came bottom of their group and failed to score a goal.

■ Alf Ramsey's England team that beat Hungary 1-0 in May 1965 featured the back six that would go on to fame with the 1966 World Cup final team – Banks, Cohen, Wilson, Stiles, Charlton, Moore – and a somewhat less iconic front five of Terry Paine, Jimmy Greaves, Barry Bridges, George Eastham and John Connelly! Know your best team, eh Alf?

■ In 1934, Italy coach Vittorio Pozzo decided to play the attacking full-back Luigi Allemandi, who had previously been banned for life after taking a 50,000 lire bribe from a crooked Torino director to throw the Torino-Juventus derby in 1927.

■ Meanwhile, fascist dictator Mussolini hand-picked the tournament referees. If you know what we mean...

★ ★ ★

▦ VITAL PUB INFO
TO FOSTER FRIENDLY RELATIONS WITH FANS OF

BRAZIL

Fanspotter's guide

All Brazilians look like those bikini-clad, flag-draped World Cup fans that lecherous TV cameramen always zoom in on. With one notable difference: in the pub, they're liable to wear even less.

Conversation starter

It's an honour to meet a person with a pubic hairstyle named after them. And a Terry Gilliam movie, too!

Accentuate the positive

The bookies don't make a team 5-1 favourites for nothing. And the five-time winners will be keen to make amends for failing against the French at the quarter-final stage in 2006.

Skirt expertly around the negative

A single bad day at the office in the Group of Death (along with Portugal and the Ivory Coast) will probably mean an early plane home. And Brazil aren't always the fastest out of the traps.

Kaká, in high visibility tabard, is yet to learn what 'Wankers' Top' actually means; Luis Fabiano and Robinho aren't about to tell him.

Form guide

Five straight wins saw Brazil qualify top of the South American group after a slightly shaky period. After lifting the Copa America in 2007, coach Dunga has timed the gelling and focus of his team to perfection.

Two to watch

Luis Fabiano has netted 25 times in 36 international outings, and is ticking along quite nicely at one every two games for Seville. He's left-footed, tough and tall, and a perfect foil for Robinho. Attacking midfielder Kaká, now with Real Madrid after six devastating years with Milan, features on *Time* magazine's list of the world's 100 Most Influential People. And you want to know if he can win a football match?

Simply the best... ever

Pelé holds the world record of 1,281 goals in 1,363 matches, a record 77 goals in 92 appearances for Brazil, and (after 18 years at Santos and two at New York Cosmos) a record 31 team trophies. He played in four World Cups, and won three. The Greatest Footballer Ever.

Useful Portuguese phrases

Você lote são um bom bocado não é? – You lot are a bit good, aren't you?
Jogando um futebol bonito, poderá ir a lugar algum. Você já ouviu falar do Arsenal? – Playing beautiful football will get you nowhere. Have you ever heard of Arsenal?
Lembre-me qual o produto que anuncia Pelé? Esqueci – Remind me which product Pelé advertises? I have forgotten.

Chat-up line

A Brazilian urban legend insists that if you do not look someone in the eye when saying 'cheers', you will have bad sex for seven years. Cheers!

This one's on me

Caipirinha, Brazil's national cocktail. It's made from cachaca, which is a liquor brewed from fermented sugar cane.

Inside line on Brazilian culture

'Wow! Brazil is big!'

(Former US President George W. Bush, having been shown Brazil on a map by Brazilian President Luiz Inácio Lula da Silva, 2005.)

Common ground

For every globetrotting Brazilian superstar that has achieved legendary status, there's another that has struggled to acclimatise to mud and big gloves in Newcastle, Manchester, Leeds...

★ ★ ★

WORLD CUP SONGS
FRANCE 1998

England United – '(How Does It Feel To Be) On Top Of The World'

(Number 9)

On the face of it, a song written by The Smiths' Johnny Marr and Bunnyman Ian McCulloch should have had potential. The mob-handed vocal didn't help, with Mac elbowed off the mic by the likes of Tommy from Space, sundry members of Ocean Colour Scene and the Spice Girls, in the final throes of not talking to each other before Geri finally quit. A plod.

It couldn't quite rekindle the beautiful vibe of football coming home for Euro 96, but Baddiel and Skinner and the Lightning Seeds' revamped 'Three Lions '98' made it to number one again. Well, it is dead good – even if the new line about 'Gazza good as before' was to prove a terrible omen when Hoddle didn't pick the big lunk. Meanwhile, at number two, Keith Allen was back with Damien Hirst, Alex James from Blur, and his own finest moment: Big Les's 'Vindaloo' was reportedly aimed at 'the stereotypical English football fan. Fat, loud, smelly, rude.'

Hmm. At least it wasn't as embarrassing as the official Scottish effort, Del Amitri's 'Don't Come Home Too Soon' – a fate-tempting 100 percent guarantee that they'd finish bottom of their group.

KOREA/JAPAN 2002

Ant & Dec – 'We're On The Ball'

(Number 3)

The Balls Brothers' original 1998 version featured a speedy ukulele-led drum'n'bass beat and a joyous ska horn part; it was rediscovered and championed by Chris Evans, and still gets played out by the Sheffield Wednesday/England Supporters Band. Ant & Dec's official retread was a slowed-down, blanded-out clicktrack affair with the usual clutter of punful namedrops and commentary samples. Bah!

There was a record seven World Cup novelties that made the charts this time around – 'The Sven Song', 'Hey Baby (We Want To See England Score A Goal)', 'Goldenballs (Mr Beckham To You)' – and many more that didn't. Fat Les's reprise roped in Ricky Tomlinson, and was easily up to Barnesy rap standards. Anyone out there remember 'Who Invented Fish & Chips? (Pop In The Onion Bag)'? Must do better for 2010, Keith...

★ ★ ★

▦ WHAT THE PAPERS SAY

2002 WORLD CUP

The official match programme for the 2002 World Cup in Japan and South Korea had a range of inspiring messages for those who were able to get there to enjoy the tournament. The programme had a sombre black cover with a plastic bumpy World Cup trophy, while inside was a rather bewildering dual Japanese/English language text.

The Prime Minister of Japan, Junichiro Koizumi, welcomes us to his country: 'I hope that you have the chance to get to meet Japanese people and through them, to learn something of our culture and traditions – possibly even visit some of our numerous sight-seeing spots.' So, all round Junichiro's for tea tonight, then... Meanwhile, Korean President Kim Dae-jung hopes: 'That the joy generated by the high-level football of this competition will have the effect of uniting the six billion strong global village.' Us too, Kim, us too. Hang on... SIX BILLION! No wonder we're running out of stuff. Not done with all the welcomes, Sio Nasu, the chairman of the organising committee, is sure that: 'Each and every match will be a truly thrilling experience.' Let's hope he didn't feel too let down by that dreadful 0-0 draw between Nigeria and England in Osaka.

Once everyone has welcomed us, we get to see an advert for a 'pocket pc' Genio, which looks more advanced than anything we have over here even now. Budweiser is also keen to unite the world with an attractive ad using different World Cup balls from history including the Mexico 70 Telstar and Argentina 78 Tango: 'One World. One Game. One Beer' ... to paraphrase Adolf Hitler.

There follows a massive section on every player from each of the 32 competing teams. Not surprisingly each player gets just two insightful and revealing lines:

The Official Programme

2002 FIFA World Cup Korea/Japan™

The designer spent over six minutes on this. The copywriter had to go and pick up his aunt from the bingo.

Seaman: Superb handler of crosses who instils confidence in the back line. Accurate positioning befitting a veteran.

Beckham: His pinpoint crosses and free-kicks are a rich source of goals. Has developed into a psychological lynchpin.

Owen: One of the world's outstanding strikers, he has a tremendous eye for goal. Lightning quick, gets behind defenders.

★ ★ ★

⊞ MOST SUCCESSFUL KIT MANUFACTURERS

To qualify, the kit must have visible branding on the outside. We have awarded 3 points for win, and 1 point for a World Cup final appearance:

- **1974** Netherlands, losing finalists – adidas 1 point
- **1978** Argentina 3, Netherlands 1 – adidas 4 points
- **1982** West Germany losing finalists – adidas 1 point

- 1986 Argentina 3, West Germany 2 – Le Coq Sportif 3 points; adidas 1 point
- 1990 Germany 1 Argentina 0 – adidas 4 points
- 1994 Brazil 0 Italy 0 (Brazil win 3-2 on pens) – Umbro 3 points; Diadora 1 point
- 1998 France 3 Brazil 0 – adidas 3 points; Nike 1 point
- 2002 Brazil 2 Germany 0 – Nike 3 points; adidas 1 point
- 2006 Italy 1 France 1 (Italy win 5-3 on pens) – Puma 3 points; adidas 1 point

They were all regarded as studs.

adidas 16 points
Nike 4 points
Le Coq Sportif 3 points
Umbro 3 points
Puma 3 points
Diadora 1 point

adidas earn their stripes...

★ ★ ★

▦ TALKING A GOOD GAME

❝

Because we don't have anything, we will do everything in our power to rebuild.

Carlos Dittborn, the president of the Organisation Committee for the Chile 1962 World Cup, after the largest earthquake ever recorded rocked Chile in May 1960

▦ VITAL PUB INFO

TO FOSTER FRIENDLY RELATIONS WITH FANS OF

NORTH KOREA

Fanspotter's guide

Not to be confused with the white-clad South Koreans, the all-red supporters of the North are laid-back, generous and right-on because they live in a Democratic People's Republic.

Conversation starter

Good job you made it down the boozer! North Korea's Supreme Leader, Kim Jong-il, has banned the World Cup from being shown back home, unless the team actually win. No live matches will be broadcast and only heavily edited highlights of North Korean victories will receive any airtime at all.

Accentuate the positive

The first Asian team to make it into the World Cup quarter-finals, in 1966, when they were cheered into a 3-0 lead against Portugal at Goodison Park by their new supporters from Middlesbrough (where they'd played their group matches)...

Skirt expertly around the negative

... They ended up losing 5-3. And that was the last time they played at the finals, until now.

Form guide

Qualified behind South Korea, but only on goal difference from Saudi Arabia, where they bravely drew 0-0 to clinch their place. Few goals conceded overall, but not many more scored. It's all immaterial, really, as this lot have no chance in the 'Group of Death' with Brazil, Ivory Coast and Portugal.

Two to watch

Interesting that plenty of the Chollima (mythical winged horses) are allowed to play abroad by the fiercely separatist state – star kid Ahn Young-Hak even plays for Suwon Bluewings in South Korea, despite the ongoing tension between the two countries! Rostov midfielder Hong Yong-Jo also looks the part.

Simply the best... ever

Pak Doo-Ik – scored the goal that beat Italy in 1966.

Useful Korean phrases

두 개의 반쪽의 게임 – It's a game of two halves.

당신은 본 적 팀 아메리카 *Team America* 그들 소금을 쳐서 훈제처럼 메이트 김 꿰매 – Have you seen that *Team America*? They stitch your mate Kim up like a kipper.

난 어쩔수없는 사랑에 공산주의, 나 – I bloody love communism, me.

Chat-up line

This is not an intercontinental nuclear missile in my pocket. However, I am pleased to see you.

This one's on me

In a rare nod to filthy capitalist ways, Taedonggang beer just made a rare venture into TV advertising. It's 'The Pride of Pyongyang', as such preferable to Makgeolli – a white rice wine, traditionally drunk by farmers.

Inside line on Korean culture

Forget Tiger Woods: according to North Korean records, Kim Jong-Il is also the world's greatest golfer. An official government handout, published on his 62nd birthday, claimed that Kim managed to scurry round a par-72 course in only 34 strokes. It also mentioned that he bagged a world record five hole-in-ones while he was at it. We don't believe it for a second, but we wouldn't say that to his face.

Common ground

One of the most successful teams in North Korea (and one for which many of the national side play their club football) is 4.25 – aka 'April 25'. Next time your team's stadium name is up for commercial sale, just remember: it could be worse. They could be named after a date in the calendar.

★ ★ ★

▦ TALKING A GOOD GAME

We don't swap shirts with animals!

Alf Ramsey after England's stormy quarter-final against Argentina in 1966

▦ (RELATIVELY) BIG FISHES

The greatest-ever players from some countries that aren't, never have been and never will be at the World Cup finals:

- Sri Lanka – Dudley Lincoln Steinwall
- Guam – Zachary Pangelinan
- Faroe Islands – Claus Bech Jorgensen
- Afghanistan – Mohammad Rohparwar
- Mongolia – Ganbaatar Tögsbayar
- Mauritius – Jacques-Desire Periatambee
- Belize – Shane Moody-Orio
- Tahiti – Felix Tagawa
- Bhutan – Wangay Dorji
- Cape Verde – Dady
- Lesotho – Lehlohonolo Seema
- Mozambique – Tico-Tico
- Eritrea – Debesai Ghierghis Ogbazghi
- Madagascar – Praxis Rabemananjara

Claus Bech Jorgensen was famous in Blackpool, as well as Tórshavn.

★ ★ ★

▦ WHATEVER HAPPENED TO THE HEROES?

Garrincha • Brazil 1958, 1962, 1966

'Garrincha' was arguably the greatest dribbler in the history of football, twice a world champion with Brazil in 1958 and 1962. In 11 years, Brazil lost only one match in which he played. And yet Manuel Francisco dos Santos was far less easy to summarise – a backward, childlike personality, born to an alcoholic father, who then almost miraculously overcame his disabilities – a deformed spine and bent legs, the left three inches shorter than the right – to become a professional athlete. There were personal problems, too. 'A womaniser like him is hard to find anywhere in the world,' said Brazilian trainer Paulo Amaral. 'When we were travelling through Europe with Botafogo, whenever we arrived at a hotel, the first thing he would do would be to ask the receptionist where we go to pay women to have sex.' As an alcoholic, he ran into problems renal, financial and marital, killing his mother-in-law in a car crash and fathering at least 14 children before he died aged just 49 in 1983.

David Harvey • Scotland 1974

There was no way back for Don Revie's famously erratic first-choice keeper Gary Sprake, when Harvey finally emerged from under his shadow in 1972-73. The seven-year understudy eventually made 445 appearances for the club between 1965 and 1985 – and there's no question that his decision to follow his dad's bloodline and play for Scotland was taken from the heart. David, now the father of seven, is a farmer and postman on Sanday in the Orkney Islands. We wish him and his family well following the news of David suffering a heart attack this January.

Tostão • Brazil 1966, 1970

Born in Belo Horizonte (a name to strike fear into English hearts) in 1947, the prolific, quicksilver forward is sometimes overlooked as a true Brazilian great, perhaps understandable given his more famous team-mates. But even Pelé can't claim to have scored 47 goals in one game as a kid! The 'little coin' went on to score 32 goals in 54 international appearances between 1966 and 1972, not to mention 366 goals in 435 Brazilian league games. In Brazil's friendly with England in the build-up to the 1970 finals, he levered himself off the ground to score the winner with an incredible scissor kick; in the real thing, he nutmegged Bobby Moore, jinked, spun and crossed the ball to Pelé to make Jairzinho's winner. Then, after scoring an incredible 71 goals in 35 league games for Vasco da Gama, he seemed to have disappeared off the face of the Earth. Finally, 25 years later, he was tracked down by the newspaper *El Globo*. He told them that Tostão no longer existed and that he now went by the name of Dr Eduardo Gonçalves de Andrade. He is now back in the fold as a TV pundit.

★ ★ ★

▦ A NON-BRAZILIAN BRAZIL XI

Brazil is possibly the only country that could field a First XI of players who play, or have played, for another country. In typical Brazilian fashion, however, they're lacking a goalkeeper:

1 Alex • Japan Moved to Japan as a 16-year-old in 1994 and qualified for Japanese citizenship in 2001. This left-sided defender played in the 2002 and 2006 tournaments.

2 Eduardo • Croatia The Rio-born striker was scouted by Dinamo Zagreb, took Croatian nationality in 2002, and then moved to Arsenal for £7.5 million in 2007. He has recovered from a badly broken leg to regain his place in the Croatian side.

3 Marcos Senna • Spain Was born in São Paulo, and moved to Villarreal CF in 2002. The midfielder took Spanish citizenship in 2006 and immediately made the Spanish squad for the World Cup in Germany.

4 Deco • Portugal Moved from Brazil to Portugal aged 19 when Benfica took an interest in him. He never played for them, but did move from Porto to Barcelona and then Chelsea. First played for Portugal in 2002 and was one of their best players in the 2006 tournament.

5 Pepe • Portugal At the age of 18, this centre-half moved from Brazil to Madeira, to play for Marítimo. Now with Real Madrid, Pepe scored the winner for Portugal against Hungary in a 2010 qualifier.

6 Kevin Kuranyi • Germany Striker born in Rio to a Panamanian mother and a German/Hungarian father. Now playing for Schalke, he walked out on the German national side and will not be selected again while Joachim Löw remains as coach.

7 Mehmet Aurelio • Turkey Moved from Flamengo to Trabzonspor in 2001, and qualified to play for Turkey in 2006. Now with Real Betis, this defensive midfielder has played for Turkey 26 times.

8 Roger Guerreiro • Poland São Paulo-born midfielder who moved to Legia Warsaw in 2006. Had his naturalisation procedure fast-tracked through to guarantee him a place in the Poland team for Euro 2008. Now with AEK Athens.

9 Zinha • Mexico Born in the Rio Grande do Norte region of Brazil, attacking midfielder Zinha made a shorter journey than the usual route to Europe, settling in Mexico. He became the first-ever foreign-born player to score for Mexico in Germany in 2006.

10 Giovani dos Santos • Mexico The son of Brazilian footballer Zizinho, Giovani opted to play for the nation of his birth, Mexico. Now at Tottenham Hotspur.

11 Francileudo dos Santos • Tunisia Zé Doca-born striker who moved to Belgium, but was not a success until he moved to Tunisia. After waiting four years for the call from Brazil he gave up, and turned out for Tunisia instead.

★ ★ ★

⊞ VITAL PUB INFO
TO FOSTER FRIENDLY RELATIONS WITH FANS OF

IVORY COAST

Fanspotter's guide

At first glance, you might think that's an orange Holland shirt. And we don't just mean the fans' replica jobs in the pub – Les Elephants play fast, fluent football.

Conversation starter

Can an African team win the World Cup on African soil?

Accentuate the positive

The top-rated African side, strong in all departments. Could be worth a punt at odds of around 25-1.

Skirt expertly around the negative

'To be honest it's a terrible group,' said Vahid Halilhodžić, the Ivory Coast coach, after watching the 'Group of Death' draw. They bombed out early in 2006, too, having being grouped with the Netherlands and Argentina.

Form guide

Unbeaten in 12 matches during the qualifying stages (along with only Spain and the Netherlands). In fact, the only points they dropped were away to Malawi, when they needed only a draw to confirm early qualification. They were beaten 3-2 by Algeria in the quarter-finals of the African Cup of Nations.

Little Bakary Koné scores against Madagascar in their World Cup qualifier in 2008.

Seven to watch

At just 5ft 4ins, Marseille's Bakary Koné is a tiny, buzzing attacker – not to be confused with his younger brother Arouna of Seville, a six-foot target man with dyed blond hair. Then there's Emmanuel Eboue and Kolo Toure at the back; ex-Spur Didier Zokora on the wing; Didier Drogba and Salomon Kalou in attack.

Simply the best... ever

Didier Drogba.

Useful French phrases

Je suis un fan de Chelsea. Je souhaite à votre pays bien – I am a Chelsea fan. I wish your country well.

Je déteste Chelsea. Je vous souhaite un retrait rapide premier tour – I loathe Chelsea. I wish you a speedy first-round exit.

Chat-up line

As the old Ivorian proverb says, 'Better a bad wife than an empty house.'

This one's on me

If you've got a sweet tooth, try Youki Soda: a sort of saccharine version of tonic water. One thing you'll want to avoid on the Ivorian menu is the *chitoum*. This is a dried black insect that tastes like dried twigs and is prepared for drying by having its guts squeezed out.

Inside line on Ivorian culture

One of Ivory Coast's biggest celebrities is reggae singer Alpha Blondy. He has written songs in protest against French President Nicolas Sarkozy, earned several Grammy Award nominations, and is widely known as the 'African Bob Marley'.

Common ground

The Ivory Coast is the world's largest producer of cocoa. Goodnight.

★ ★ ★

▦ IT'S A CRIME

A bit of a Pickle

On Sunday 20 March, almost four months before the 1966 World Cup began, England suffered the huge embarrassment of having the Jules Rimet trophy stolen from under their noses at a stamp exhibition at the Methodist Central Hall in Westminster. Luckily for the nation, a small black and white mongrel dog called Pickles sniffed the trophy out of a garden hedge in Beulah Hill, South Norwood.

Pickles' owner, David Corbett, said: 'Even when I starting taking off the paper and saw it was a statue, nothing really stirred. Then I noticed it said Brazil, West Germany and so on and ran in to my wife immediately. It wasn't very World Cuppy though... very small.' As a reward Pickles was invited to the World Cup winners' banquet and got to lick the plates clean. Sadly, he choked on his lead in pursuit of a cat a year later.

Blame it on Rio

The Jules Rimet trophy was stolen again, on 19 December 1983, when it was taken from a display at the Brazilian Football Confederation headquarters in Rio de Janeiro. Although the front of the cabinet was made of bulletproof glass, the back was wooden and easily prised off with a crowbar. The trophy has never been recovered, and it is presumed that it was melted down for its gold by opportunist thieves. American photographic company Eastman Kodak had a replica commissioned and presented it to the President of Brazil in 1984.

Cold comfort

After their 1978 World Cup defeat to Peru, Scotland's Willie Johnston was found to have taken a cold remedy containing the banned stimulant fencamfamin, and was sent home, and banned for life from playing for his country. Sometimes it's better to put up with a sniffle.

Moore trouble

England's preparations for the 1970 World Cup took a bizarre turn when captain Bobby Moore was placed under house arrest on suspicion of stealing a gold and emerald bracelet from the Green Fire jeweller's shop in the Tequendama Hotel in Bogotá, Colombia. The preposterous claim that he had trousered the $600 bracelet was made by Alvaro Suarez. Moore was released to play in the tournament in Mexico and later cleared of all wrongdoing in court. Police believed that Moore was set up by Suarez, with the cooperation of a shop assistant.

Maradona's medicine

Diego Maradona tested positive for ephedrine during the USA 94 tournament, but a few months before that it was clear that all was not quite right with the Argentinian enigma. TV footage had emerged of him crouched behind a Mercedes, taking pot shots at the press assembled round his front gates with an air rifle. Several journalists were injured and Maradona eventually received a three-year suspended sentence.

Korean cuisine

'It was beyond all doubt that the incident was a product of a deliberate act perpetrated by adulterated foodstuff as they could not get up all of a sudden just before the match.' They might have sacrificed a bit of grammar in the translation, but North Korea's statement after their 1-0 defeat to South Korea in a 2010 qualifier was clear... those dastardly South Koreans had poisoned their boys before the game. Kim Joo-sung of the South Korean FA's cool reply was: 'The statement sets a high political tone, not about the sport itself. There's no need to respond to it.' The North Koreans refused to let doctors take blood tests and FIFA took no further action.

The winners of the worst placard ever made sense to themselves but nobody else.

A Politburo penalty

Eduard Streltsov is considered to be one of the most talented Russian players who ever lived, earning the nickname 'the Russian Pelé'. He had won an Olympic gold medal with the Soviet Union side in Melbourne in 1956 and seemed set to make an impact on the World Cup, when his life was put on hold in 1958. Streltsov was accused of raping a 20-year-old woman, though the evidence against him always seemed murky. He had recently upset a high-ranking member of the Politburo, Ekaterina Furtseva, after snubbing her daughter's advances, and appeared to have his card marked for making anti-Soviet comments. Streltsov was offered a deal: plead guilty and you'll be released to play in the 1958 World Cup. He admitted his guilt, and was sentenced to 12 years in a labour camp. He was released after five years, and resumed his place in the Torpedo Moscow and USSR sides, but never quite reached his former heights, having been badly injured by a fellow prisoner.

Joining the wrong side

Algerian-born Alex Villaplane captained France in the first World Cup in 1930 and claimed that leading his adopted nation out against Mexico in Montevideo was 'the happiest day of my life'. During the Second World War, however, Villaplane was head of a very different team – becoming an SS sub-lieutenant of the Nazi-controlled Brigade Nord Africain. They committed many atrocities in the Périgord region. When the Allies liberated Paris in 1944, Villaplane stood trial and, found guilty, was executed by firing squad.

The Football War

In 1969, El Salvador and Honduras met in two World Cup qualifying matches on 8 and 15 June. Between the two games, La Guerra del Fútbol, a four-day war, broke out between the two nations. Simmering tension over immigration issues was magnified by the football matches; riots turned into war, with both sides launching bombing raids on each other and the Salvadoran army commencing a land offensive against Honduras. After 100 hours a ceasefire was called, with some 3,000 people dead. Incredibly, the two protagonists then had to meet each other in another game eleven days after the war, in a play-off in Mexico City. El Salvador won 3-2 and made it to Mexico for the final tournament.

Escobar's own goal

When Colombian defender Andrés Escobar scored an own goal in the 1994 World Cup against hosts USA, it had fatal consequences. Colombia lost the game 2-1 and came bottom of Group A. Ten days later, after returning home, Escobar was shot six times outside El Indio bar, in Medellín by Humberto Muñoz Castro. It was never clear whether Castro was part of a syndicate who lost heavily when Colombia were knocked out in the first round. Castro was sentenced to 43 years in prison, but was released after just 11 years.

★ ★ ★

HOW THE WORLD CUP HAS GROWN (MOSTLY)

1930

■ **13 competitors**

Seven from South America, two from North America and four from Europe took part in the inaugural World Cup finals, with no qualification process. Belgium, France, Romania and Yugoslavia were eventually persuaded to travel to Uruguay from Europe.

The Uruguayan World Cup side take a local bus to a game. Expect England to do the same in South Africa.

1934

■ **16 competitors**

Thirty-two teams entered the tournament and the qualification process whittled this down to 16. Champions Uruguay declined to enter, in retaliation for Europe's lack of interest four years earlier.

1938

■ **15 competitors**

Thirty-seven teams entered, competing for 16 places in the finals. Having qualified, Austria withdrew because they had been absorbed by Germany and their place was not offered to another nation, so 15 contested the finals tournament. Spain did not enter due to the civil war, and Argentina and Uruguay were still protesting about FIFA's perceived bias towards Europe.

1950

■ **13 competitors**

In the aftermath of the Second World War, many countries had neither the means nor the will to summon up a football team for the tournament and although qualification thinned 34 teams down to 16, only 13 teams took part. The Germans and Japanese were banned, not surprisingly. And three countries qualified but then didn't take their places: Turkey withdrew for financial reasons; Scotland refused to travel as runners-up to England in qualifying; and India turned down their place because FIFA rules meant they couldn't play in bare feet.

1954
to 1978

■ **16 competitors**

A period of stability followed, with 16 countries travelling to each tournament. As the game spread across the globe, the number of initial entrants continued to rise: 45, 56, 56, 74, 75, 99, 107.

1982
to 1994

■ **24 competitors**

The competition was expanded from 16 to 24 teams to allow more representation from North America, Africa and Asia. In all, 109 teams entered in 1982, 121 in 1986, 116 in 1990 and 147 in 1994.

1998
to 2010

■ **32 competitors**

The final tournament was expanded again, with 32 qualifying from an ever-increasing field of 174. By 2002 this had risen to 199, but that dipped to 197 for 2006. And, just when you began to think FIFA had run out of countries, 204 entered for South Africa 2010.

★ ★ ★

▦ VITAL PUB INFO
TO FOSTER FRIENDLY RELATIONS WITH FANS OF

PORTUGAL

Fanspotter's guide

There's something just a little bit retro about the green piping on Portugal's new Nike kit. Have a sneaky look when you come across gaggles of happy Iberian girls with the red shirt tied in a knot above their navels.

Conversation starter

Lordy, just how cute is that Pepe? Surely the cutest player at the World Cup.

Accentuate the positive

Fourth place in 2006, third place in 1966.

Skirt expertly around the negative

Failed to qualify for every other finals in history except 1986 and 2002, when they were summarily knocked out in round one.

Form guide

Ooyer, the Portugeezers cut it close in qualifying, losing to Denmark and getting pegged back by Sweden and even Albania. But when the chips were down, they won their last five matches, including both legs of a tense play-off against Bosnia-Herzegovina.

Three to watch

Cristiano Ronaldo is number one in an excellent trio of Spanish-based players that includes Real centre-back Pepe (often deployed in midfield by Portugal boss Carlos Queiroz) and Malaga winger Edinho. But, balancing the ebullient youth and new faces on the international scene, Portugal also boast an enviable mix of experience.

Simply the best... ever

Eusebio, the so-called 'Black Pearl', was the leading scorer at the 1966 World Cup. The Mozambiquian still hangs around with the national team, where he is considered a lucky talisman.

Useful Portuguese phrases

Você é muito sortudo de estar aqui – You are very lucky to be here.

Desculpe-me por meu amigo. Ele tem bebido demais – I'm very sorry about my friend. He has had far too much to drink. Hic.

Chat-up line

The olive skin, the beautiful black hair held back by bands and ribbons. You remind me a bit of Cristiano Ronaldo. In a good way, like. (Best not follow up by asking if she's a Lisboan.)

This one's on me

Port (it's like sherry only a bit classier. From Porto. Hence the name. Port, that is, not sherry.)

Inside line on Portuguese culture

The proud national characteristic is *saudade*, a profoundly nostalgic mindset which can easily see a football fan fall to his/her knees at the rose-tinted memory of pulling on Sporting Lisbon's funny stolen Celtic kit. Go for the kill with a packet of Spangles.

Things we have in common

Yes, yes: there are four Portuguese currently playing for Chelsea, all now over 30, and Nani is at Man U, but did you know that ex-Birmingham City centre-forward Bob Latchford was once boss of Portuguese second division team FC Belenenses, based in Belem, Lisbon?

★ ★ ★

▦ YOU'VE BEEN HAD
WORLD CUP HOAXES

If you're all going França...

In the run-up to the 1998 World Cup, a whole country's crushing disappointment at failing to qualify was lifted by a single radio report. Portuguese listeners nationwide heard the fantastic news that Iran had been forced to pull out of that summer's World Cup in France because of security issues. And that the country pulled out of FIFA's velvet ball-bag as a replacement was... Portugal! Thousands went to work and school in a state of fervoured ecstasy. Millions then reminded them that the date was 1 April.

The hoax that won the World Cup

The editor of German satirical magazine *Titanic* claims to have personally won the right to host the 2006 World Cup for Germany. Back in July 2000, Martin Sonneborn sent prank faxes to seven FIFA committee members at their Zurich hotel, timed to coincide with a crucial vote. The football fat-cats were promised a cuckoo clock, a beer mug and 'a fine basket with specialities from the Black Forest' – and duly ignored the fancied South Africa as hosts, choosing Germany against all the odds. Sonneborn has since written a book entitled *I Did It For My Country*. It details how the German FA held a €300 million lawsuit over his head, making him swear never to try to influence another FIFA decision. Bloody ingrates!

The 1958 World Cup was a hoax!

The Swedish conspiracy-theory documentary *Konspiration 58* is football's equivalent of *Capricorn One*. Instead of exposing the NASA moon landings as a fake, the 2002 TV special sensationally proved that the 1958 World Cup in Sweden never really took place. And it must have been true, because stars of the day and even UEFA bigwig Lennart Johansson all admitted it. Apparently, the finals were mocked up by TV and radio companies, working in league with the CIA and FIFA. It was all part of Cold War strategy, aiming to test just how far the truth could be stretched by the media. As if an economically backward country like Sweden could stage a major sporting event! Even though it was revealed at the end to be a mockumentary hoax, many viewers mistook the retraction for yet more political chicanery, and went on believing.

Pity Heinz Kwiatkowski – facing up to the most prolific goalscorer in any World Cup, Just Fontaine; getting kicked in the crown jewels by his right-back – and it was all a fake. What the f---?

★ ★ ★

⊞ ALL IN THE GAME

From simple blow football, via the lavish 'Munich' edition of Subbuteo, to the startlingly realistic Xbox 360 and PlayStation 3 games, many attempts have been made to bring the World Cup into your home. But nothing satisfies quite like Top Trumps, where the World Cup '78 game we had threw up the following great head-to-heads:

⊞ Deyna • Poland

World Cup Appearances 7, beats

⊞ Archie Gemmill • Scotland

World Cup Appearances 1.

⊞ Marius Treson • France

Height 6'0" draws with

⊞ Sepp Maier • West Germany

Height 6'0".

⊞ Alberto Rivelino • Brazil

World Cup Goals 6, beats

⊞ Ali Parvin • Iran

World Cup Goals 0.

⊞ Claudio Gentile • Italy

International Appearances 14, loses to

⊞ Kenny Dalglish • Scotland

International Appearances 49.

⊞ Johan Neeskens • Netherlands

World Cup Goals 9, beats

⊞ Daniel Killer • Argentina

World Cup Goals 0.

1978 Top Trumps. Three things you need to know: One, when holding an Archie Gemmill (Scotland) card do not, repeat NOT, go for the height category. Two, when holding Ali Parvin (Iran) go for caps not goals. And three, get bonus points for noticing that Deyna (Poland) – Legia Warsaw and Man City – has his name mis-spelled on the card.

Scotland

Archie Gemmil

World Cup Appearances	1
World Cup Goals	0
International Appearances	23
International Goals	2
Height	5'5"

Poland

Denya

World Cup Appearances	7
World Cup Goals	3
International Appearances	93
International Goals	40
Height	5'11½"

Argentina

Daniel Killer

World Cup Appearances	0
World Cup Goals	0
International Appearances	19
International Goals	2
Height	6'2"

West Germany

Sepp Maier

World Cup Appearances	12
World Cup Goals	0
International Appearances	79
International Goals	0
Height	6'0"

Iran

Ali Parvin

World Cup Appearances	0
World Cup Goals	0
International Appearances	81
International Goals	19
Height	5'7"

★ ★ ★

▦ 2010 WORLD CUP
WHO CAME LAST?

One problem with the World Cup is that there is too much focus on who wins. We wanted to establish who managed to finish last of the 207 nations affiliated to FIFA – and it gets quite competitive at the bottom.

190th • Andorra

Goals for 3; goals against 39 in 10 matches. Unlike some of the teams we have ranked below them, these results were achieved in a qualifying group rather than in a preliminary round, so arguably they fared better than their rival world minnows. Ranked 202nd by FIFA.

191st • San Marino

Goals for 1; goals against 47 in 10 matches. Ranked 203rd, the (equal) worst team in the world arguably overachieve, just by a) turning up and b) getting whupped in their qualifying group.

192nd • Lesotho

Minus 16 in the goal stakes, and that was in the preliminary qualifiers. Ranked 150 by FIFA, these boys really underachieved!

193rd • Seychelles

Minus 17 and counting.

194th • Mauritania

Goal difference of -19.

195th • Djibouti

No points and a goal difference of -28 in their six preliminary qualifiers.

196th • American Samoa

Arguably the worst showing of any team in the world in the preliminary qualifiers, losing 7-0 at home to neighbours Samoa and 15-0 at home to Vanuatu. Ranked 203rd equal by FIFA.

197th • Anguilla

The worst single result worldwide in the preliminary qualifiers, losing 16-0 to El Salvador.

198th • Palestine

Failed to turn up for the away leg of

Romell Lumbs of Anguilla is left trailing by El Salvador's Shawn Martin. The only time he touched the ball was after his keeper got tired of picking it out of the net.

their preliminary qualifier against Singapore. They were already 4-0 down from the home leg, and the 3-0 result awarded by FIFA was probably better than they would have actually achieved. The Palestine Football Federation appealed for a reschedule on the grounds that its players couldn't get permits to leave the Gaza Strip, but FIFA turned a deaf ear.

199th • Guam

Withdrew from the competition without playing a game in the Asian qualifying group.

200th • Central African Republic

201st • São Tomé and Príncipe

Almost incredibly, the African preliminary draw was conducted one day before the format of the qualifiers was announced, so good work there, CAF. A knockout format was (eventually) put in place for the ten lowest-ranked teams. São Tomé and Príncipe were drawn against the Central African Republic, and both withdrew in early September 2007. Gah, if only one of them had held on, they'd have got a bye into the big time!

202nd • Eritrea

The 'Red Sea Boys' managed to get their application form in, but withdrew before the African preliminary matches had even been arranged.

203rd • Papua New Guinea

Failed to meet the registration deadline for the South Pacific Games (which also acted as a preliminary World Cup qualifier in Oceania). FIFA ranks them 203rd equal.

204th • Bhutan

Also failed to register in time, but were at least trying to do so. FIFA took pity and added their 196th-ranked team into the Asian preliminary qualifiers draw – only for them then to withdraw without playing a match. There's gratitude for you. We've bumped them down the list for their crap attitude.

205th • Brunei

206th • Laos

207th • Philippines

All members of FIFA, all failed to register for the World Cup by the close of entries on 15 March 2007. Which kinda makes it a waste of time being in FIFA in the first place. Pathetic. FIFA 165-ranked Philippines are the most pathetic of the lot, on our reverse alphabetical order rule.

★ ★ ★

▦ VITAL PUB INFO
TO FOSTER FRIENDLY RELATIONS WITH FANS OF

SPAIN

Fanspotter's guide
They're the ones in red with yellow trim, looking brassed off 'cos they've just been knocked out again.

Conversation starter
Win Spanish friends and influence Spanish people by giving them a greeting gift – *El Caganer* (lit: 'The Pooing Man'). These scatological statues (or 'scatues', if you like) have been staples of Nativity scenes for

The royal warrant was on the base.

eons, but are mostly sold nowadays in the guise of famous film stars, celebrities and even footballers. The figurine of Cristiano Ronaldo with his pants down, in Number Two mode, is one of the biggest sellers. Shame it's not so popular in Brazil: Kaká and Dunga fit the bill perfectly.

Accentuate the positive
Euro 2008 champions, with no less than nine Spaniards being chosen for the UEFA Team of the Tournament. It was a victory that put them top of the FIFA world rankings...

Skirt expertly around the negative
... They therefore became the only team ever to hit world No 1 without having won a World Cup.

Form guide
Unbeaten in qualifying, with their fine showing at the 2009 Confederations Cup contributing to two world records (for 15 consecutive wins and 35 consecutive unbeaten games) which they then went and lost – to the USA! Since qualifying, they have beaten Armenia, Bosnia-Herzegovina, Argentina and Austria in friendly matches.

Three to watch
Argentine Lionel Messi may be the reigning European Player of the Year, but many rate his Barcelona midfield team-mates Xavi (third place) and Andres Iniesta (fourth) more crucial to the success of the Catalan giants. Remember Iniesta's incredible late strike against Chelsea in last season's Champions

League semi? Meanwhile, there's no disputing that Valencia's David Villa is on fire upfront with 35 goals in 54 internationals.

Simply the best... ever

Today, it seems odd that the great Barça and Inter inside-forward Luisito Suarez played only 32 times for his country, stretched between 1957 and 1972 (scoring 14 goals). He's the only Spaniard ever to win European Footballer of the Year, in 1964.

Useful Spanish phrases

Estoy hablando de hechos – I am talking about facts. (A good one to throw in if the conversation turns to Rafa Benitez.)

Él tiene el cuerpo de un hombre, sino la cara de la dama! – He has the body of a man but the face of a lady! (A good one to throw in if the conversation turns to Fernando Torres.)

Son follada – They are f*cked. (A good one to throw in conversation turns to Liverpool FC.)

Chat-up line

No me importa mirar, pero prefiero no participar – I don't mind watching, but I'd rather not join in.

This one's on me

Sangria all round! – lemonaded down, as is traditional on the Costa del Sol, to around 1.5 percent alcohol.

Inside line on Spanish culture

Every year, many wine-producing villages in Spain hold an enormous and extremely messy 'grape battle' to mark the end of the harvest. This involves the villagers hurling all the leftover grapes at each other until a) the grapes are all gone, or b) someone finally says, 'hold on – what the hell are we doing?'

Common ground

The guitar was invented in Andalucia, originating from Arab lutes. In the 1790s, the sixth string was added. So, essentially, the Spanish are to blame for your mop-headed teenage neighbour who spends three hours every evening tunelessly dismantling and reassembling 'Stairway To Heaven' on his second-hand Gibson. So cheers for that.

★ ★ ★

WORLD CUP SONGS
GERMANY 2006

Embrace • 'World at Your Feet'

(Number 3)

Hmm. An extremely U2-ish band with a rather average U2-ish single. But hold on! On the sly, it's almost as if these long-haired Yorkshire blokes have usurped our hope for a chanty anthem with a cunning tale of popping their cherries. 'You're the first in my life / To make me think that we might just go all the way / And I want you to know we're all hanging on.' You wouldn't have caught Bobby Moore and the lads mouthing that filth back in the day. For some reason, thousands of elderly pop stars tried their hand at a novelty hit this time around, the best being from those cheeky West Ham wideboys and one-time punk rock sensations Sham 69 & The Special Assembly with a rework of their 'Hurry Up Harry' pub anthem, aka 'Hurry Up England'. Not so sure about Tony Christie's '(Is This The Way To) The World Cup', chiefly because 'The World Cup' never even looked like it was going to rhyme with 'Amarillo'. At least The Laddz mastered that basic requirement with their cheap Bangles rehash, 'Chant Like an English Fan'. And then there was 1960s warbler John Leyton and his audacious attempt at a comeback with 'Hi-Ho Come on England'. Time to call it a day...

★ ★ ★

TALKING A GOOD GAME

Cameroon's Charles Ntamark, on the eve of Argentina's little upset at Italia 90

> It may be that I am marking Maradona in the opening match. We know all about him, but he doesn't know anything about me.

⠿ WHAT THE PAPERS SAY
2006 WORLD CUP

The official programme cost €10 and had a clear message to give for the world, with some big slogans: 'Opponents, Not Enemies', 'A Dream Goes Around the World', 'A Time to Make Friends…'

It also had some penetrating questions for the stars. David Beckham is asked: 'What would you pay to hold the FIFA World Cup in your hands on 9 July?' His response leaves no room for doubt that he does actually want to win the tournament: 'I would pay a lot. Probably as much as I could afford.'

There's also room for some slightly surreal content, including a long conversation between the adidas Telstar from 1974 and the new +Teamgeist Berlin: 'Every night I have the same wonderful dream,' says the 2006 ball. 'Free kick for Brazil, Ronaldinho whispers "My baby, baby, balla, balla," he then strokes me, puts me down, runs at me, and his instep sends me on a dream trip towards the goal – after a soft landing in the net I wake up.' Quite literally, the programme was talking balls here.

But FIFA also kept its focus where it should always be: on the money. They took out a full-page ad appealing for help against 'ambush marketing'. 'These "ambushing companies" don't invest one penny to support the event – they simply try to "cash-in". Do not bring any such promotional fan items with commercial branding from these "ambushing" companies into the stadium.'

★ ★ ★

⠿ WINNERS OF THE GOLDEN BOOT AWARD

This award is given to the leading scorer in each tournament. The following players have won:

■ 1930 Uruguay	Guillermo Stábile	Argentina	8 goals
■ 1934 Italy	Oldrich Nejedly	Czechoslovakia	5 goals
■ 1938 France	Leônidas da Silva	Brazil	7 goals
■ 1950 Brazil	Ademir	Brazil	9 goals
■ 1954 Switzerland	Sándor Kocsis	Hungary	11 goals
■ 1958 Sweden	Just Fontaine	France	13 goals

■ 1962 Chile	Garrincha	Brazil	4 goals
	Vavá	Brazil	4 goals
	Leonel Sánchez	Chile	4 goals
	Dražan Jerković	Yugoslavia	4 goals
	Valentin Ivanov	Soviet Union	4 goals
	Flórián Albert	Hungary	4 goals
■ 1966 England	Eusébio	Portugal	9 goals
■ 1970 Mexico	Gerd Mueller	West Germany	10 goals

Was Mueller light on his toes? You betcha.

■ 1974 West Germany	Grzegorz Lato	Poland	7 goals
■ 1978 Argentina	Mario Kempes	Argentina	6 goals
■ 1982 Spain	Paolo Rossi	Italy	6 goals
■ 1986 Mexico	Gary Lineker	England	6 goals
■ 1990 Italy	Salvatore Schillaci	Italy	6 goals
■ 1994 USA	Hristo Stoichkov	Bulgaria	6 goals
	Oleg Salenko	Russia	6 goals
■ 1998 France	Davor Šuker	Croatia	6 goals
■ 2002 S Korea/Japan	Ronaldo	Brazil	8 goals
■ 2006 Germany	Miroslav Klose	Germany	5 goals

★ ★ ★

▦ VITAL PUB INFO
TO FOSTER FRIENDLY RELATIONS WITH FANS OF

SWITZERLAND

Fanspotter's guide

Swiss shirts are red and white Puma jobbies, but fans are more likely to dress, chant and drink like neutrals.

Conversation starter

Brilliant work by the Swiss at the last World Cup: the first team ever to get sent packing without letting in a single goal!

Accentuate the positive

There hasn't been a war in Switzerland since 1515.

Skirt expertly around the negative

Must have something to do with those Swiss Army knives. They're terrifying. Just terrifying. Invented in 1897, some of the more sarcastic military historians have suggested that its inclusion of a nail file, toothpick and small set of tweezers has been instrumental in turning the Swiss Army into one of planet earth's most feared and dangerous fighting forces.

Form guide

It wasn't the toughest of qualifying groups, but the Schweizer Nati finished ahead of Greece, Latvia and Israel. It'll be tougher against Spain, Honduras and Chile, but we fancy the Swiss for second place.

These will not be encouraged inside stadiums in 2010.

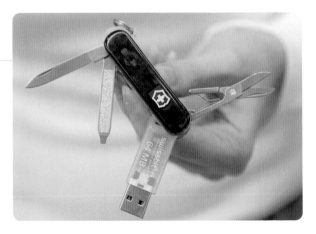

Two to watch

All-time record goalbanger Alexander Frei of FC Basel is the most likely headline writer in the Swiss team. And you'll remember the name (and maybe the hair?) of Lucerne's dynamic midfielder Hakan Yakin from England games over the past decade.

Simply the best... ever

Stéphane Chapuisat made his name as a free-scoring marksman for Borussia Dortmund in the 1990s, when he was regularly Swiss Player of the Year.

Useful French/German phrases

Sollte ich spreche zu Ihnen in Deutsch oder Französisch?/Devrais-je vous parler en Français ou en Allemand? – Should I address you in French or German?

Deutsch ist, dann – German it is, then.

Francais il est, donc – French it is, then.

Ironischerweise, jetzt habe ich festgestellt haben, welche Sprache Sie sprechen, habe ich entdeckt habe ich nichts zu sagen. Ich entschuldige mich für die Aufnahme Ihrer Zeit/ Ironiquement, maintenant, j'ai créé la langue à m'adresser à vous en, j'ai découvert que je n'ai rien à vous dire. Je m'excuse d'avoir pris votre temps – Ironically, now I have finally established which language to speak to you in, I have discovered I have nothing to say to you. I apologise for taking up your time.

Chat-up line

Maybe suffrage was extended to Swiss women only in 1970, but you get my vote.

This one's on me

Hot chocolate. Or – if you're feeling adventurous/suicidal – a pint of fondue.

Inside line on Swiss culture

'You know what the fellow said – in Italy, for thirty years under the Borgias, they had warfare, terror, murder and bloodshed, but they produced Michelangelo, Leonardo da Vinci and the Renaissance. In Switzerland, they had brotherly love, they had five hundred years of democracy and peace – and what did that produce? The cuckoo clock.'

(Orson Welles as Harry Lime in *The Third Man*, 1949)

Common ground

Cape Verde-born midfielder Gelson Fernandes is now with Saint-Étienne after a couple of seasons at Manchester City, where he was signed by Sven-Göran Eriksson, who called him the 'best young player in Switzerland' and Arsenal stopper Philippe Senderos is currently on loan with Everton.

★ ★ ★

▦ NOT-SO-NICE NAMES

■ Giuseppe Bossi (Switzerland, 1934)
■ Tom Lynch (USA, 1934)
■ Hans Mock (Germany, 1938)
■ Alfredo Foni (Italy, 1938)
■ Roger Byrne (England, 1954)
■ Jerzy Gorgon (Poland, 1974)
■ Daniel Killer (Argentina, 1978)
■ Alan Rough (Scotland, 1978)
■ Mark Hateley (England, 1986)
■ Bryan Gunn (Scotland, 1990)
■ Onandi Lowe (Jamaica, 1998)
■ Kieron Dyer (England, 2002)
■ Robbie Fowler (England, 2002)
■ Stern John (Trinidad & Tobago, 2006)
■ Loco (Angola, 2006)

A Stern test for Frank Lampard, as England took on Trinidad & Tobago in the 2006 World Cup

★ ★ ★

▦ WHATEVER HAPPENED TO THE HEROES?

Sándor Kocsis • Hungary 1954

Kocsis was one of the most potent strikers ever seen on a football field, particularly fearsome in the air. He played for the 'Magnificent Magyars' (who gave England a memorable lesson in 1953, becoming the first foreign side to win at Wembley in a stunning 6-3 victory), and at club level for Ferencváros and Honvéd in his native Hungary, then for Barcelona up until his retirement in 1965. His incredible 75 goals in 68 internationals outstrips even the record of Gerd Mueller, these two marksmen alone posting a long-term career goal ratio above 1.00 (though it's worth noting that Kocsis' team-mate Ferenc Puskás comes third on 0.99, not so far behind the 1.103 of 'Golden Head'). He was top scorer in the 1954 World Cup with 11, which included two of his seven international hat-tricks. But, tragically, his coaching career was cut short in the 1970s when he was diagnosed with leukaemia. In 1979 he fell to his death from a fourth-floor window of a hospital in Barcelona.

Dan Petrescu • Romania 1994, 1998

Sándor Kocsis celebrates another goal, as he helps Hungary beat Uruguay in the 1954 World Cup semi-final.

Hounded at every step in Britain for his resemblance to Fox Mulder of *The X-Files* (and a name that sounds so amusingly like 'Pet Rescue'), the slippery wing-back was probably quietly pleased to head back to Romania after eight years of titters at Sheffield Wednesday, Chelsea, Bradford City and Southampton. At home, he's an all-time great, having won 95 caps. He lost out in a penalty shoot-out in the quarter-finals in 1994; while in 1998, the whole Romanian team dyed their hair blond after losing a bet to coach Anghel Iordanescu, before being defeated by Croatia in the second round. He's now shaping up as a great coach. After stints at Rapid Bucharest, Sportul Studentesc and Wisla Kraków, he led little Unirea Urziceni to the Liga 1 title in 2009 and the Champions League. Late in 2009, his name was even linked with the job of Scotland manager. However, he moved instead to Russian First Division side Kuban Krasnodar.

★ ★ ★

▦ TALKSPORT'S ALL-TIME BEST SCOTLAND WORLD CUP XI

1 Alan Rough 624 games for Partick Thistle, 53 Scotland caps, and 16 clean sheets for Scotland. He came on in his last-but-one international, deputising for Jim Leighton after he'd lost his contact lenses. Scottish goalies, eh?

2 Danny McGrain The legendary full-back played at the 1974 World Cup – despite being diagnosed with diabetes – and then skippered Scotland at Spain 82. Had a strange start to his career, when he was overlooked by Rangers scouts who wrongly assumed he was Catholic!

3 David Hay Had a busy summer in 1978, starring in the World Cup team, making a dream £225,000 move from Celtic to Chelsea, then getting trapped in a warzone on holiday when the Turkish army invaded Cyprus!

4 Tommy Docherty The Doc played at centre-half in Scotland's first-ever finals in Switzerland in 1954. Sadly for Scotland and Tommy, they were trounced 7-0 by Uruguay and were soon on a flight home.

5 Alan Hansen Only 26 caps to his name when many – excluding Jock Stein and Alex Ferguson – would've made him first name on the teamsheet ahead of Willie Miller and his Aberdeen mukka Alex McLeish.

6 Billy Bremner Tigerish midfielder for Leeds United and Scotland who finally made it to a World Cup in 1974, nine years after his international debut. Bremner led Scotland through three group games unbeaten in West Germany, but goal difference did for them, and home they went. Sadly, a distinguished international career ended with a life ban after a busy night involving a Copenhagen nightclub brawl and an upside-down bed.

7 Kenny Dalglish The most-capped Scottish footballer and, arguably, the best. King Kenny played for Scotland in the 1974, 78 and 82 tournaments, but never quite reproduced his fantastic club form for Celtic and Liverpool. He did score the equaliser in the classic 3-2 win against the Netherlands, however.

8 David Narey Scored a fantastic long-range goal against Brazil in Spain 82 to put Scotland 1-0 up. Sadly this just served to rattle the Brazilians' cage and they thrashed the Scots 4-1.

9 Joe Jordan 'Jaws' minus his two front teeth was a frightening prospect, and always an inspiration to the Scots. Strong both in the air and on the floor and toughened up in the Leeds school of hard knocks.

10 Denis Law The King was a Scotland great, but reached a World Cup finals only in the twilight of his career. Ninety minutes against Zaire in 1974, and sadly that was it for the great man.

11 Willie Johnston It's easy to overlook Bud's brilliance just because of his banned stimulant scandal at WC78 and his less-than-proud record of being sent off 22 times. Trickiness personified!

★ ★ ★

▦ **VITAL PUB INFO**
TO FOSTER FRIENDLY RELATIONS WITH FANS OF

HONDURAS

Fanspotter's guide
Los Catrachos will be all white on the night.

Conversation starter
America Ferrera, the bird out of *Ugly Betty*, was born in LA to Honduran parents.

Accentuate the positive
Honduras didn't let themselves down on their only previous finals appearance, drawing 1-1 with both Spain and Northern Ireland.

Skirt expertly around the negative
After all, you don't want to end up fighting a Football War, as Honduras did with El Salvador in 1969, when border tensions were sparked by World Cup qualifiers.

Wilson Palacios: not bothered about playing for a small team in white against a bigger local rival.

Form guide
Can Colombian coach Reinaldo Rueda continue to drill the rest of the Honduran team so as to capitalise on their potentially potent front line? They qualified close behind the USA and Mexico in the CONCACAF region, beating off opposition from previous finals makeweights Jamaica, Trinidad & Tobago and Costa Rica.

Two to watch
David 'The Panther' Suazo is probably the best striker from the whole of

Central America, currently plying his deadly opportunist trade at Inter after eight years at Cagliari. Then there is Wilson Palacios of Spurs, of course.

Simply the best… ever

Carlos Pavon is now 36 but still pivotal up front, the all-time Honduran top-scorer with 56 goals in 95 internationals. He's played mostly in Mexico, with spells in Italy and Spain.

Useful Spanish phrases

¿Juegas un partido de dobles? – Would you like to play a game of doubles? (Useful if you get chatting to Honduran twins at the bar).

Una pista – A slippery slope.

Chat-up line

In another life you must have been Mayan princess. And, for you, I'm prepared to make sacrifices.

This one's on me

Guaro tastes like liquorice; *chicha* is a home-brew made out of pineapple skin.

Inside line on Honduran culture

Belize, previously known as British Honduras, is the only Central American country with a British colonial heritage. Honduras, meanwhile, is Spanish Honduras. But if they happen to win, we'll claim full credit.

Common ground

The magnificently named Carlo Costly has been on fire recently, scoring eight in Honduras's last 16 internationals. Mr Costly plays in Poland for GKS Belchatów, and went on loan to Birmingham City in 2009. Meanwhile, Wigan Athletic boast two Honduran internationals in stopper Maynor Figueroa and midfielder Hendry Thomas (who turns out to be 'The Panther' Costly's somewhat less predatory cousin) – not forgetting Wilson Palacios at Spurs.

★ ★ ★

▦ TALKING A GOOD GAME

Where's Pak Seung-Zin? My granddad's told me to get his autograph.

A six-year-old Middlesbrough fan, as the surviving members of North Korea's side returned to Middlesbrough – scene of their 1966 win over Italy – in 2002

▦ TEN WORLD CUP VENUES NO LONGER WITH US

1 Stadio delle Alpi, Turin, Italy, 1990-2009

Built for Italia 90, it hosted Brazil v Sweden, Brazil v Costa Rica, Brazil v Scotland, Argentina v Brazil, and the semi-final between England and Germany. It was unpopular with Juventus fans due to poor sight lines, so the decision was made to rip it down and start again.

They should have knocked the bloody thing down after the England-Germany semi-final in 1990.

2 Estadi de Sarrià, Barcelona, Spain, 1923-97

The home ground of RCD Espanyol, this stadium was the venue for all three Group C matches in 1982: Argentina v Italy, Argentina v Brazil and the classic encounter when Italy beat Brazil 3-2. It was destroyed in 1997 when Espanyol moved to a new stadium.

3 Rheinstadion, Düsseldorf, Germany, 1925-2000

The home ground of Fortuna Düsseldorf hosted Sweden v Bulgaria, Sweden v Uruguay, Yugoslavia v West Germany, West Germany v Sweden, and Sweden v Yugoslavia in the 1974 tournament. It was demolished to make way for a new stadium.

4 Roker Park, Sunderland, England, 1898-1997

Sunderland's ground hosted three games in Group 4 in 1966 – Italy v Chile, Soviet Union v Italy, and Soviet Union v Chile. It was also used for one quarter-final – Soviet Union v Hungary. Roker Park was knocked down in

1997 when Sunderland moved to the Stadium of Light. A housing estate now stands on the site.

5 Ayresome Park, Middlesbrough, England, 1903-95

Middlesbrough's home hosted three games from Group 4 during the 1966 tournament: Soviet Union v North Korea, Chile v North Korea, and the Koreans' incredible 1-0 win over Italy. Ayresome Park was demolished in 1997 to make way for houses when Boro moved to the Riverside Stadium.

6 White City Stadium, London, England, 1908-85

The owners of Wembley Stadium refused to cancel a greyhound racing night for a piffling matter like the World Cup, so White City had to be used for one game in 1966 – the 2-1 victory for Uruguay over France was watched by 45,000 fans. Built for the 1908 Summer Olympics, the stadium was demolished in 1985 to make way for BBC White City.

God knows the state of the White City pitch, but if the stadium were a dog it would have been put down.

7 Hardturm, Zurich, Switzerland, 1929-2008

The home of Grasshopper-Club Zurich was the venue for Hungary's 9-0 demolition of South Korea in the 1954 finals, and West Germany's 7-2 trouncing of Turkey, as well as Austria's victories over Scotland, Czechoslovakia and Uruguay. It was demolished to make way for a new stadium in 2008.

8 Stadio Giorgio Ascarelli, Naples, Italy, 1930-42

A multi-purpose sports stadium that hosted two games during the 1934 World Cup: Hungary's 4-2 win over Egypt in the first round and the third-place play-off between Germany and Austria. It was destroyed beyond repair by an Allied bombing raid in 1942.

9 Stadio Nazionale del PNF, Rome, Italy, 1927-53

The National Stadium hosted three matches in the 1934 tournament: Italy v United States, Czechoslovakia v Germany, and the final between Italy and Czechoslovakia. The ground was flattened in 1953 when Lazio and AS Roma both moved to the Olympic Stadium.

10 Estadio Pocitos, Montevideo, Uruguay, 1921-33

Home to Peñarol, the Pocitos was the scene of the first ever World Cup goal in 1930, when Lucien Laurent scored for France in the 19th minute of their game against Mexico. It also staged Romania v Peru. It was demolished in 1933 when Peñarol moved to the Estadio Centenario.

★ ★ ★

NICKNAMES

■ Garrincha   The Brazilian legend was born Manuel Francisco dos Santos. His brother gave him the name Garrincha ('little bird') because of his mis-shapen legs, the result of childhood polio. In Brazil he was also known as Anjo de Pernas Tortas ('Angel with Bent Legs').

■ Der Kaiser   Before a friendly game for Bayern Munich in Vienna, Franz Beckenbauer posed for a photograph beside a bust of former Austro-Hungarian emperor Franz Joseph I and the media christened him 'Der Kaiser'.

■ El Buitre   Emilio Butragueño of Spain was known as El Buitre ('the Vulture'). So named for his habit of feeding off the scraps created by members of the La Quinta del Buitre ('the Vulture's Cohort'), five home-grown youngsters who went on to form the core of the Real Madrid side in the early 1980s.

He may have had a dodgy pair of legs, but Garrincha was one of Brazil's all-time greats.

Puskas always made sure he was in peak physical condition.

■ **Bello di Notte** Zbigniew Boniek, who starred for Poland in the 1978, 82 and 86 tournaments was dubbed the 'Beauty of the Night' by the Juventus president Gianni Agnelli because he appeared to excel himself in evening games.

■ **The Galloping Major** Ferenc Puskás picked up his moniker because he played for Honvéd, the Hungarian army team. When he moved to Real Madrid he acquired a new nickname, Cañoncito Pum ('the Booming Cannon').

■ **Dutch style** In the 1970s, the Netherlands didn't just play some terrific football, they came up with some of the best nicknames, too. Agile winger Robbie Rensenbrink was dubbed het Slangenmens ('the Contortionist') while his team-mate Willy van de Kerkhof was Stofzuiger ('the Vacuum Cleaner').

■ **El Loco** Peru's keeper Ramon Quiroga was known as 'the Crazy One', because occasionally he got bored in goal and joined in the game further upfield.

Sadly, players' nicknames tend to be rather less descriptive and poetic in England. Osvaldo Ardiles was known as 'Pitón' ('Python') in Argentina, but became 'Ossie' when he arrived at White Hart Lane. Tom Finney was 'the Preston Plumber', because he came from Preston and was a plumber; Bryan Robson was known as 'Captain Marvel', while Paul Ince nicknamed himself 'the Guv'nor'. Usually, however, the acorn doesn't fall far from the tree when it comes to nicknames: Paul Gascoigne is 'Gazza', Glenn Hoddle is 'Glenda' or 'Hodds'; and David Beckham isn't 'the Tattooed Angel', or 'Man Who Wears a Sarong', but just 'Becks'.

★ ★ ★

▦ THE WORLD CUP UP THE PICTURES

The following is a list of the official FIFA World Cup films and their narrators:

- 1954 Switzerland – German Giants
- 1958 Sweden – Hinein! – Herbert Zimmermann, Heribert Meisel and Heinz Gottschalk
- 1962 Chile – Viva Brazil
- 1966 England – Goal! – Nigel Patrick
- 1970 Mexico – The World at Their Feet – Patrick Allen
- 1974 West Germany – Heading for Glory – Joss Ackland
- 1978 Argentina – Campeones
- 1982 Spain – G'olé! – Sean Connery
- 1986 Mexico – Hero – Michael Caine
- 1990 Italy – Soccer Shoot-Out – Edward Woodward
- 1994 USA – Two Billion Hearts – Liev Schreiber
- 1998 France – La Coupe de la Gloire – Sean Bean
- 2002 S. Korea/Japan – Seven Games from Glory – Robert Powell
- 2006 Germany – The Grand Finale – Pierce Brosnan

Mexico 1970: With the world at his feet, England's Norman Hunter had a different definition of the phrase 'hard as nails'.

★ ★ ★

▦ TALKING A GOOD GAME

"

Simon Barnes,
The Times

The 1986 World Cup has already brought us a new approach to the game. Let us call it *los bastardos* football...

⠿ VITAL PUB INFO

TO FOSTER FRIENDLY RELATIONS WITH FANS OF

CHILE

Fanspotter's guide
Red with white go-faster flashes.

Conversation starter
I notice [bitter local rivals] Peru finished bottom of the South American qualifying group. Serves them right for falsely claiming to have invented the 'Chilena', or bicycle kick.

Accentuate the positive
Coach/national hero Marcelo Bielsa did a great job getting Chile through the qualifiers for the first time in 12 years...

Skirt expertly around the negative
... His nickname is El Loco ('The Madman'), and the Argentinian was responsible for his home country's first-round flop in 2006.

Form guide
Second in the CONMEBOL qualifiers, just one point behind Brazil.

One to watch
Alexis Sánchez, the so-called 'Wonder Boy' ('El Niño Maravilla'). Now 21, Udinese's ultimate tricky dribbler has already won over 30 international caps.

Simply the best... ever
Inter's Ivan Zamorano was a real eyecatcher at France 98 – and as top scorer helped Chile to their best-ever major tournament finish – bronze at the 2000 Olympics.

Useful Spanish phrases
¿Por qué se llama Chile, cuando en realidad es muy caliente? – Why is it called 'Chile' when it's actually quite warm?

Lo siento. Esa es una vieja broma – I am sorry. That's an old joke.

No te sientas mal que no se puede hablar Inglés. Que no falta nada – Do not feel bad that you cannot speak English. You are not missing anything. (Useful whenever Alan Hansen is speaking.)

Chat-up line
Chile is the longest country in the world, boasting a latitude equivalent to the distance between Scotland and Nigeria. It's not all about length, though, is it?

This one's on me

Pisco – a liquor distilled from grapes.

Inside line on Chilean culture

Chile's national dance is the *cueca*: men and women act out the thrill of the chase, and you can guess who acts all coy behind their white handkerchiefs. Note: when the ladies wave the hankies in the air, it doesn't signal total submission.

Common ground

Many of the teams in the Chilean league have names that reveal their founders. In the current Chilean top flight (Primera Division de Chile), you'll find 'Everton' playing alongside 'Rangers'. You've got to feel for the Old Firm: they've been working towards that for years.

The linesman was frequently ridiculed for excessively camp offside decisions.

★ ★ ★

▦ TALKING A GOOD GAME

Geoff Hurst in *1966 And All That* (2001)

" Was it a goal? Did the ball cross the line? Those two questions have haunted me for most of my adult life. They are the questions I am asked most often – and I don't know the answers.

▦ CHAMPAGNE/SOUR MILK MOMENTS

Uruguay 1930

■ **Hero** Hector Castro, who scored Uruguay's winning goal in the 1930 final, had only one hand. He had lost one hand and part of his arm in a childhood accident.

■ **Zero** When the ref awarded a foul against the USA in their semi-final v Argentina, their physio invaded the pitch to protest and threw his bag onto the ground. He smashed a bottle of chloroform, was overcome by the fumes, and had to be carried off.

Italy 1934

■ **Hero** Italian coach Vittorio Pozzo, who fashioned a World Cup-winning side under the oppressive presence of Mussolini's fascist regime.

■ **Zero** England, for not entering a tournament they had a decent chance of winning.

France 1938

■ **Hero** Austrian striker Matthias Sindelar refused to play for the new 'Greater Germany', making himself an enemy of the Gestapo in the process. He was found dead in his apartment alongside his girlfriend the following year under suspicious circumstances.

■ **Zero** Benito Mussolini, who sent the telegram message '*Vincere o morire*!' ('Win or die') to Italy's team before the final against Hungary in Paris. Though, in fairness to the murderous fascist dictator, this was later explained as a rousing 'Victory or Bust!' sort of message and it seemed to help the cause as Italy won.

Brazil 1950

■ **Hero** Alcides Ghiggia, who had the brass nerve to score Uruguay's winner, in what was effectively the final, in front of nearly 200,000 football-mad Brazilians at the Maracana.

■ **Zero** All the Brazil fans who committed suicide after that defeat. Come on... it's only a game, isn't it!

Switzerland 1954

■ **Hero** West Germany who, trailing 2-0 to a brilliant Hungarian side who had defeated them 8-3 earlier in the tournament, somehow managed to turn the final round and win 3-2.

■ **Zero** The Hungarian Communist regime, who made life unbearable for some of the returning Hungarian side who lost the final they had been expected to win.

Sweden 1958

■ **Hero** Just Fontaine, who scored a record 13 goals for France in just six games.

■ **Zero** Brazilian officials who hadn't bothered with packing a change strip. When Sweden won the toss to play in yellow in the final, a set of blue shirts were purchased and badges taken off the yellow shirts and hurriedly sewn on to the new ones. They won anyway.

Chile 1962

■ **Hero** Tournament organiser Carlos Dittborn did a superb job in rebuilding the damaged stadia and infrastructure after a devastating earthquake in 1960. Sadly, Dittborn died a month before the start of the tournament that he had worked so hard to make possible.

■ **Zero** Italian journalists Antonio Ghirelli and Corrado Pizzinelli, who wrote about Santiago in such unflattering terms that their words led to the Battle of Santiago.

England 1966

■ **Hero** Who else but Geoff Hurst, the only player ever to score a hat-trick in a World Cup final.

■ **Zero** The thieving git who stole the Jules Rimet trophy. Thought to be petty thief Edward Betchley, who attempted to collect a ransom for it. The supposed £15,000 in a suitcase presented to him by Detective Inspector Charles Buggy of the Flying Squad was mostly cut-up newspapers and Betchley was nicked and charged with breaking and entering, and the theft of the trophy.

Mexico 1970

■ **Hero** The whole Brazil team – playing football at its very best.

■ **Zero** The rent-a-mob Mexicans who, on the eve of the Brazil game, kept the England players awake all night singing and drumming outside their hotel.

West Germany 1974

■ **Hero** Netherlands, for their glorious Total Football, even though they fell at the final hurdle.

■ **Zero** The weather… it tipped it down for most of the tournament.

Argentina 1978

■ **Hero** Mario Kempes, whose six goals for the host nation, including two in the final, ensured Argentina's World Champion status for the first time.

■ **Zero** Argentina, who took gamesmanship to a new level before the final. They kept the Netherlands waiting for seven minutes before emerging from

The Argies also insisted that the Dutch played with no keeper.

the tunnel; and then objected to the plastercast worn by René van de Kerkhof on his right wrist. At one stage the Dutch side, led by Johan Neeskens, left the field, before the matter was resolved.

Spain 1982

■ **Hero** Disgraced Italian striker Paolo Rossi, who bounced back from a betting scandal and two-year suspension. His six goals, including a hat-trick against Brazil, were a major factor in Italy winning the World Cup in Spain.

■ **Zero** The police in Madrid who, aggrieved on behalf of their Argentinian cousins over the Falklands, took their frustrations out on England fans with their batons, regardless of whether they were behaving themselves or not.

Mexico 1986

■ **Hero** Diego Maradona, who hauled a fairly average Argentina side all the way to the trophy.

■ **Zero** Spanish goalkeeper Andoni Zubizarreta for his comedy moment against Northern Ireland. Coming out to meet a ball that had been punted harmlessly forward, he completely sliced his clearance sending the ball straight up into the air. Fortunately a defender was on hand to help out and he nodded the ball gently to Zubizarreta. The keeper then slipped and fell over allowing Colin Clarke to head the ball into an empty net. Fortunately for Zubizarreta, Spain won the game 2-1.

Italy 1990

■ **Hero** England's Paul 'Gazza' Gascoigne. His tears defined not just the moment when the whole English nation began to take an interest in the game – by October he was on the front of the bed-wetting anti-sport music bible the *Melody Maker* – but it was also the moment when the decade began. The definitive film is yet to be made, but it has all the ingredients of a classic – triumph, failure, disaster, sex, drugs, domestic violence and erm... folk music ('Fog On The Tyne' anybody?). A one-man industry with no man in charge. In essence, both a hero and a zero.

■ **Zero** West Germany and Argentina, who played out a dreadful non-event of a final, notable only for two dismissals and a dodgy penalty.

USA 1994

■ **Hero** The American public who, despite the misgivings of more traditional football countries, made this the best supported tournament ever.

■ **Zero** Diego Maradona whose demented, frothing charge towards the TV camera after his goal against Greece in the first round rather gave the game away. He was sent home in disgrace after a drug test proved positive for ephedrine.

Gullit, Gascoigne and Rijkaard all became managers – with varying degrees of success.

France 1998

■ **Hero** French coach Aimé Jacquet, who blended together a French side capable of becoming World Champions, despite the pressure of being hosts.

■ **Zero** Saudi Arabia's coach Carlos Alberto Parreira. Four years earlier he coached Brazil to the trophy, this time round he was sacked before the Group stage had ended.

Japan/South Korea 2002

■ **Hero** German keeper Oliver Kahn's performances carried a fairly average German side all the way to the final. He let in just three goals in Germany's seven games and became the only goalkeeper ever to win the FIFA World Cup Golden Ball for best player of the tournament.

Oliver was a Kahn-do kinda guy.

■ **Zero** In time added on at the end of the Group C game between Brazil and Turkey, Turkish defender Hakan Ünsal booted the ball at Rivaldo, who was waiting to take a corner. The ball hit the Brazilian just above the knee, but he fell dramatically to the turf holding his face. Ünsal was dismissed, but Rivaldo was fined 11,670 Swiss Francs by FIFA after they viewed the video evidence.

Germany 2006

■ **Hero** Brazil's Ronaldo scored his 15th World Cup goal in the 3-0 win against Ghana, claiming a new record.

■ **Zero** French legend Zinédine Zindane, for signing off from international football by headbutting Italian defender Marco Materazzi in the chest during the final. He commented afterwards: 'I'm a man, and I'm telling you that I would rather have been punched in the face than have heard those words. But I heard them, and I reacted.'

★ ★ ★

▦ NOT NEEDED ON VOYAGE

The 18 England players who didn't make it to Spain in 1982 when
Ron Greenwood trimmed his squad from 40 to 22 were:

- Gary Bailey – Manchester United
- Alan Devonshire – West Ham United
- Derek Statham – West Bromwich Albion
- Steve Perryman – Tottenham Hotspur
- Cyrille Regis – West Bromwich Albion
- Garth Crooks – Tottenham Hotspur
- Alvin Martin – West Ham United
- Dave Watson – Stoke City
- Russell Osman – Ipswich Town
- Tommy Caton – Manchester City
- Dennis Mortimer – Aston Villa
- Sammy Lee – Liverpool
- Eric Gates – Ipswich Town
- Tony Morley – Aston Villa
- Peter Barnes – Leeds United
- Paul Goddard – West Ham United
- Gary Shaw – Aston Villa
- David Armstrong – Southampton

Of these players, only Gary Bailey
and Alvin Martin had more luck
when Bobby Robson named his
squad for the 1986 tournament.

Tony Morley and
Gary Shaw would be
disappointed to miss
out in 1982, but at
least neither of them
looked like Peter Withe.

★ ★ ★

▦ STAN COLLYMORE'S ULTIMATE AND IMPOSSIBLE WORLD CUP PUB QUIZ

ANSWERS

1 It was a Home International match against Wales, played at Ninian Park, Cardiff, in October 1949, which also counted as a World Cup qualifier. They won 4-1, 'Wor' Jackie Milburn notching a hat-trick. (England's first home World Cup qualifier was at Maine Road, Manchester the following month, a 9-2 victory over Northern Ireland.)

2 Scotland's first World Cup action came against Northern Ireland in Belfast. The Scots trounced the Irish 8-2.

3 Never. Not a good omen for Argentina, as Messi is the current incumbent.

4 His name was Paul Nicolas.

5 Eight, by fatal heart attack.

6 The Maracana was still partly a building site; the changing rooms were flooded, and a false wooden floor had been put in for the players' comfort. Unfortunately, it was a foot higher than the original, so when Metic was performing his pre-match calisthenics, he hit his head on an exposed beam and knocked himself out.

7 Jeff Astle, a notoriously bad traveller.

8 Zaire. The police intervened to halt the coach on its way south on the autobahn.

9 The Moroccan players were only just drifting on to the pitch when he started the second half. The goalie Allal Ben Kassou arrived in his penalty area just in time to save a goalbound shot.

10 Brazilian referee Almeida Rego blew for time six minutes early, but could only restart the match much later after he'd cleared the crowd from the pitch. France had been pushing for an equaliser, but Argentina ended up 1-0 victors.

11 Two. Ironically, it was the first indoor World Cup match ever (played at the Pontiac Silverdome in Michigan).

Sub 1,600 revolvers.

★ ★ ★

▦ WORLD CUP 2010 FIXTURES

Group A

Date	Time	Team 1	Team 2	Venue	Result
Fri 11 June	3.00	South Africa	Mexico	Johannesburg, SC	
Fri 11 June	7.30	Uruguay	France	Cape Town	
Wed 16 June	7.30	South Africa	Uruguay	Pretoria	
Thu 17 June	7.30	France	Mexico	Polokwane	
Tue 22 June	3.00	Mexico	Uruguay	Rustenburg	
Tue 22 June	3.00	France	South Africa	Bloemfontein	

FINAL TABLE

Team	P	W	D	L	F	A	Pts
1.							
2.							
3.							
4.							

Group B

Date	Time	Team 1	Team 2	Venue	Result
Sat 12 June	3.00	Argentina	Nigeria	Johannesburg, EP	
Sat 12 June	12.30	South Korea	Greece	Port Elizabeth	
Thu 17 June	3.00	Greece	Nigeria	Bloemfontein	
Thu 17 June	12.30	Argentina	South Korea	Johannesburg, SC	
Tue 22 June	7.30	Nigeria	South Korea	Durban	
Tue 22 June	7.30	Greece	Argentina	Polokwane	

FINAL TABLE

Team	P	W	D	L	F	A	Pts
1.							
2.							
3.							
4.							

Group C

Date	Time	Team 1	Team 2	Venue	Result
Sat 12 June	7.30	England	USA	Rustenburg	
Sun 13 June	12.30	Algeria	Slovenia	Polokwane	
Fri 18 June	3.00	Slovenia	USA	Johannesburg, EP	
Fri 18 June	7.30	England	Algeria	Cape Town	
Wed 23 June	3.00	Slovenia	England	Port Elizabeth	
Wed 23 June	3.00	USA	Algeria	Pretoria	

FINAL TABLE	Team		P	W	D	L	F	A	Pts
	1.								
	2.								
	3.								
	4.								

Group D

Date	Time	Team 1	Team 2	Venue	Result
Sun 13 June	7.30	Germany	Australia	Durban	
Sun 13 June	3.00	Serbia	Ghana	Pretoria	
Fri 18 June	12.30	Germany	Serbia	Port Elizabeth	
Sat 19 June	3.00	Ghana	Australia	Rustenburg	
Wed 23 June	7.30	Ghana	Germany	Johannesburg, SC	
Wed 23 June	7.30	Australia	Serbia	Nelspruit	

FINAL TABLE	Team		P	W	D	L	F	A	Pts
	1.								
	2.								
	3.								
	4.								

Group E

Date	Time	Team 1	Team 2	Venue	Result
Mon 14 June	12.30	Netherlands	Denmark	Johannesburg, SC	
Mon 14 June	3.00	Japan	Cameroon	Bloemfontein	
Sat 19 June	12.30	Netherlands	Japan	Durban	
Sat 19 June	7.30	Cameroon	Denmark	Pretoria	
Thu 24 June	7.30	Denmark	Japan	Rustenburg	
Thu 24 June	7.30	Cameroon	Netherlands	Cape Town	

FINAL TABLE	Team		P	W	D	L	F	A	Pts
	1.								
	2.								
	3.								
	4.								

Group F

Date	Time	Team 1	Team 2	Venue	Result
Mon 14 June	7.30	Italy	Paraguay	Cape Town	
Tue 15 June	12.30	New Zealand	Slovakia	Rustenburg	
Sun 20 June	12.30	Slovakia	Paraguay	Bloemfontein	
Sun 20 June	3.00	Italy	New Zealand	Nelspruit	
Thu 24 June	3.00	Slovakia	Italy	Johannesburg, EP	
Thu 24 June	3.00	Paraguay	New Zealand	Polokwane	

FINAL TABLE

Team	P	W	D	L	F	A	Pts
1.							
2.							
3.							
4.							

Group G

Date	Time	Team 1	Team 2	Venue	Result
Tue 15 June	3.00	Ivory Coast	Portugal	Port Elizabeth	
Tue 15 June	7.30	Brazil	North Korea	Johannesburg, EP	
Sun 20 June	7.30	Brazil	Ivory Coast	Johannesburg, SC	
Mon 21 June	12.30	Portugal	North Korea	Cape Town	
Fri 25 June	3.00	Portugal	Brazil	Durban	
Fri 25 June	3.00	North Korea	Ivory Coast	Nelspruit	

FINAL TABLE

Team	P	W	D	L	F	A	Pts
1.							
2.							
3.							
4.							

Group H

Date	Time	Team 1	Team 2	Venue	Result
Wed 16 June	12.30	Honduras	Chile	Nelspruit	
Wed 16 June	3.00	Spain	Switzerland	Durban	
Mon 21 June	3.00	Chile	Switzerland	Port Elizabeth	
Mon 21 June	7.30	Spain	Honduras	Johannesburg, EP	
Fri 25 June	7.30	Chile	Spain	Pretoria	
Fri 25 June	7.30	Switzerland	Honduras	Bloemfontein	

FINAL TABLE	Team	P	W	D	L	F	A	Pts
	1.							
	2.							
	3.							
	4.							

Round of 16

Date	Time	Team 1	Team 2	Venue	Result
1. Sat 26 June	3.00	Winner Gp A	2nd Gp B	Port Elizabeth	
2. Sat 26 June	7.30	Winner Gp C	2nd Gp D	Rustenburg	
3. Sun 27 June	3.00	Winner Gp D	2nd Gp C	Bloemfontein	
4. Sun 27 June	7.30	Winner Gp B	2nd Gp A	Johannesburg, SC	
5. Mon 28 June	3.00	Winner Gp E	2nd Gp F	Durban	
6. Mon 28 June	7.30	Winner Gp G	2nd Gp H	Johannesburg, EP	
7. Tue 29 June	3.00	Winner Gp F	2nd Gp E	Pretoria	
8. Tue 29 June	7.30	Winner Gp H	2nd Gp G	Cape Town	

Quarter-finals

Date	Time	Team 1	Team 2	Venue	Result
C. Fri 2 July	3.00	Winner 5	Winner 7	Port Elizabeth	
A. Fri 2 July	7.30	Winner 1	Winner 3	Johannesburg, SC	
B. Sat 3 July	3.00	Winner 2	Winner 4	Cape Town	
D. Sat 3 July	7.30	Winner 6	Winner 8	Johannesburg, EP	

Semi-finals, Third place play-off and Final

Date	Time	Team 1	Team 2	Venue	Result
Tue 6 July	7.30	Winner A	Winner C	Cape Town	
Wed 7 July	7.30	Winner B	Winner D	Durban	
Sat 10 July	7.30	Third place play-off		Port Elizabeth	
Sun 11 July	7.30	FINAL		Johannesburg, SC	

All kick-off times BST